Emotional Abuse:

Silent Killer of Marriage

A 30-Year Abuser Speaks Out

Austin F. James

austin.f.james@gmail.com

What People are Saying About

"Emotional Abuse: Silent Killer of Marriage"

"This is the book that opened my eyes to the truth of my marriage. I bought it on a Saturday, read it over the weekend and found the name of a counsellor on Monday. Over the years I stopped being a woman and became a workhorse, stopped being a person and became an appliance. Every hobby and interest was sabotaged or made so difficult to pursue that I gave up. Things I valued were `accidently' broken, lost or discarded until I gave up valuing anything at all. This book also explained what happened to my husband; how he was a little man at 12, painting the exterior of his mother's house, and supporting her since he was 16. After reading this book I realise it was all doomed from the start but I thought if I just tried harder, was nicer, did something different all would be okay. I am over walking on eggshells, keeping out of his way and being blindsided by explosive rages and unreasonable demands directed at me without reason or warning. I am over being belittled, bullied, blamed and abused. This book was the catalyst for me seeing the truth."

H Muggins

"From an abused wife of 29 years (now divorced): Mr. James validated the ups, downs, and very unbalanced life of the abused while explaining the not-so-conscious behavior of the abuser. While not knowing him, I believe that his journey and change is real based on his willingness to expose himself and share all of the steps in his own recovery. Steps that I watched and waited for. I believe this book offers hope for those that are willing to see it and it validates the experience of the abused (when many others don't recognize it.) If you are curious about emotional abuse or if you think that you or a friend are involved in it (abused or abuser), this book does give insight, and points towards help."

MS Lily

"...one of the most heartfelt, deeply moving stories I've read in a long time. The first words that came to my mind as I read his book were, "Insurmountable Courage." For it had to have taken him raw courage to write about such an emotional journey. James' honesty and candor are evident throughout. He paints powerful images of emotional/verbal abuse, and details the step-by-step recovery he went through, while offering a helping hand to others who suffer, or who are in pain and suffering as he and his family suffered. He apologizes for his part in the abuse throughout the book, yet offers tremendous help to the abuser and the abused alike."

C Kaelin

Contents

Introduction

Guilt is the very nerve of sorrow. __Horace Bushnell

My name is Austin James. I was an emotional abuser for 30 years. I am presently 5 years into my recovery. Life is good!

My hope is this book will make a difference in someone's life or marriage, regardless of which side of the emotional abuse equation they may find themselves on.

It has been on my heart for a while to share my marriage experience and the emotional abuse that destroyed it in the hopes someone, maybe you, can relate your experience to mine and find hope and hopefully, the path that leads to healing... in whatever form that may consist of.

I feel my journey needs to be told, not because it, or I, or my wife are mega-important, or allowing you to be a voyeur within a small window of our marriage and relationship makes for that great of a read.

No, it needs to be told because with the aid of five years hindsight with a *much* healthier mind, I witness emotional and verbal abuse in a surprisingly great number of relationships and marriages, yet rarely is it "outed" for what it is—a silent killer.

I say *silent* because abuse is rarely talked about outside the confines of the relationship or marriage. I have witnessed repeatedly emotional abuse occurring in front of family members or close friends yet, just as in my own abusive marriage, not a word is spoken about what is happening. At least not to the ones involved face anyways.

For that reason, I've labeled emotional abuse as a *silent killer* of marriages.

Is emotional or verbal abuse, at some levels, accepted by society? After all, who of us hasn't thrown a verbal barb or two at someone, a loved one, when we've been hurt? Who has not yelled and said hurtful things or put someone else down? We know those behaviors in isolated instances do not necessarily define one as an abusive person, only human.

Therefore, perhaps we tend to look the other way when we see this behavior done to others. When we see a reoccurring pattern of verbal barbs or put downs from someone, does it merely get labeled as a character flaw, or "It's just the way they are," rather than what it is, abuse—a psychological disorder?

There's no doubt any of us would get involved if we saw physical abuse taking place, yet do we choose to ignore emotional abuse because we mistakenly think the 'blows' of words or actions aren't just as damaging to the victim?

Many times the victims of abuse try to merely cope and *hope* things will change and get better. Maybe if they would "try harder," do "more things right," or "give a little more" to the relationship things would calm down and improve; the victims begin to buy into the lie that somehow they are to blame.

Perhaps the victims of abuse chooses to stay silent out of shame or guilt or because so much of the abuse happens behind closed doors. Maybe deep down inside no one feels abusive behavior can be altered, that an emotionally sick person *can* be healed.

I'm living proof that is not true.

Many deep psychological hooks, webs, traps, patterns, and behaviors are developed and ingrained during the time of abuse that's for sure. Decoupling, untangling or trying to make sense of the mess is not an easy task and normally best left to professionals.

The mind is a terribly complex organ, no doubt, and I'm certainly NOT qualified to try to explain its makeup or its workings. Nor am I qualified to speak as to why as a society we have seemed to turn our backs on this dysfunction that affects so many people and families. It is clearly an epidemic.

What I do feel qualified to say, however, is as long as the ones impacted by abuse - giver, receiver, family, or friend - choose to stay quiet and make excuses, try to cope, or simply wish and hope for things to change, this silent killer, and its devastating effects are destined to repeat themselves through our lives, the lives of our children, and our children's children for generations to come.

The epidemic of low self-worth, broken lives, broken children, and broken families will continue to spread just as cancer does, killing everything it touches along the way.

So if I, one who has caused incalculable devastation in the lives of the people I love the most, can somehow bring forth discussion or perhaps the start of healing by sharing with you my experiences and thoughts as an emotional abuser, than the pain of reliving the past, and the misery it brought on me is worthwhile.

It's the least I can do.

As I look back, I'm mortified at the person I was for nearly two-thirds of my life but it's an inescapable fact. The recovery will last the rest of my days I suppose. Some abusive patterns are dead, but some are deeply entwined in my soul and psyche and therefore, constantly "nip at my heels."

On rare occasions, I resort back to a form of the person I used to be. The major difference today is when those patterns of behavior re-emerge, I'm now consciously *aware* of them and can take corrective action FAST—that's the plan anyways.

As I continue to travel further away from the man I was and journey towards the man I am to be, I have discovered there isn't much written from the perspective of the abuser. Perhaps if we, the ones who wounded mercilessly, are willing to step forward and say, "I am he" or "I am she," more awareness of this epidemic will take place and over time, the killer known as emotional abuse can be stopped or minimized greatly.

It's important to realize as you read what follows, I had *no idea* what or who I was during all the years I was abusive, as amazing as that may seem to a healthy mind. I'm amazed at that fact myself, but I was *completely* blinded to the man I became.

Nor did my wife and I once hear the question "abuse?" come up during years of seeing both secular and Christian counselors, even though 'anger' was *always* brought up as the underlying issue in our marriage problems.

To this day, I'm completely floored by those two facts yet it seems to add more credibility to the word 'silent' in "silent killer."

Whether through these pages you are about to confirm who you are, or were, or are about to see your spouse, boyfriend, girlfriend or significant other, I want to tell you there IS hope. Recovery and healing from abusive behavior *can* happen. I'm proof and I've witnessed others who have been set free as well, even after decades of destructive behavior.

Abuse is a psychological disorder that usually has its roots traced back to an earlier traumatic event during the childhood years, when the brain has not developed to the point of being able to cope with such trauma. One simply is not born abusive. It is a learned behavior and anything learned can be unlearned by those willing.

Yes, recovery is a long and painful road to travel at times, but it is well worth the journey. Wounds *can* heal... slowly. New, healthy patterns can be formed and those patterns, working through you and your spouse, can transfer to your children, regardless of their age.

So perhaps this book will give you time to pause and reflect before you take that next step. Maybe it will cause you to seek help from professionals who are not afraid to talk "abuse" and are willing to help you attack this silent killer, head-on, before it has further opportunity to destroy within your life or home.

On the other hand, maybe that has already occurred and you're reading this in an attempt to further heal the wounds abuse has inflicted deep within you that NO ONE can know except you.

Either way, I wish you good luck and God's protection on your journey.

It's important to note that I'm not a doctor, psychologist, or counselor, nor have I played one on TV. I hold no degree in the sciences of the mind.

I simply have a thirty-plus year *Degree in Life* as an abusive man. My experiences I talk about; the way I went about my recovery and what I learned are *my* experiences alone and may not align with conventional wisdom amongst professionals—so be it.

The methods I used worked for me and I am confident some of what you will read in these pages will work for you too—IF you are ready.

Emotional abuse is a *very* complex situation. To be frank, it is not just the abuser that needs helped. Most times the one abused has suffered some type of dysfunction during their childhood that has allowed them to be controlled, or put in situations where abuse can take root.

Many times the victims of abuse had a hard time with setting boundaries *before* they came into the abusive relationship. This in no way implies that victims of emotional abuse are to blame IN ANY WAY for the abusive behavior - they are not! Nor is the one being abused enabling the abuser.

An abuser is going to abuse because they are broken within. The victim of abuse didn't do anything to 'turn on' the abuse, and they aren't doing anything now to 'enable' the abuse.

Turning things around is best left to the pros for sure, or someone who has professional training and practical application in the area of emotional abuse.

I do not intend in any way to recommend or suggest what you are to do in *your* situation - your situation is unique to you just as mine was to me.

However, some basic characteristics of emotional abuse and the relationships it touches certainly have common underlying themes across all situations.

My hope is this book will allow you to possibly see patterns in your own life or the life of someone close to you, which you can take and start a dialog, or perhaps find a professional who is familiar with emotional abuse to help you.

This is simply my story in all its gory detail, at least as much of it as I can remember. Yes, I hope there is therapeutic help in these pages, but please don't take anything I say as professional advice, okay? We are just friends talking here and some things must be taken with a grain of salt.

In closing, the very fact you are reading my words defines me as an "author" (a fledgling one *at best*). I felt it more important to take a leap of faith and get my story *out there,* rather than sharpen my literary skills *prior* to writing this book.

I'm sure this will be a work in progress and only you, as the rightful judge, will determine if I made the right decision in coming forward with my experiences and what I've learned from them. I ask for your grace to cover the literary mistakes made through the pages that follow and simply *dive-in* to the experiences you're about to read.

Let's get on with it shall we?

Austin

Chapter 1
Transformation

Let no man trust the first false step of guilt: It hangs upon a precipice, whose steep descent in lost prediction ends. __Young

In twenty-four years of marriage to my wife, Teri, there was a lot of pain, sprinkled with some incredibly good times, *incredibly* good. To coin a phrase from a favorite movie of mine, when times were good, Teri and I "went together like peas and carrots." These words, of course, said with the appropriate Forrest Gump southern drawl.

We flat had a blast together.

Nevertheless, the pain reached a crescendo one day in April years ago when my wife finally hit the wall and told me she wanted to end our marriage.

Ending the marriage wasn't something either of us took lightly. Of course, divorce should *never* be taken lightly. We, as Christians, believed in the sanctity of marriage and the Word of God. Moreover, there were two children (age 17 & 19) involved as well.

However, I suppose there comes a time when enough is enough and core beliefs can sometimes take a backseat to the realities of a relationship. Years of emotional abuse, arguing and trying repeatedly to fix the same problems over and over finally took its toll. The marriage, from my wife's eyes, was terminal and divorce seemed to be her only option.

Though this phase of my life's journey didn't have the ending I was hoping and praying for - a total reconciliation with Teri prior to divorce, I do hold out great hope one day I'll witness the things that are very important to me namely, a loving wife, a great home, and children who grow up to be healthy and helpful to themselves, their spouse, and their community.

The journey, since that dreadful day hearing those dreadful words of divorce years ago, and today, have been the most incredible journey of my life! A journey that has taken me to the revelation of being an emotionally abusive man, husband and father, to the despair of suicidal thoughts (twice!), and finally, to the incredibly delightful discoveries of learning how much my Lord and Savior (for me it's Jesus Christ) loves me.

On that note, though I don't intend to cram God or Christ down anyone's throat, the truth is after spending the first forty years of my life as an atheist, I realized 14 years ago that for me, Jesus is the way... the only way. Though I cannot nor will not deny Him (for his grace is what set me free from this bondage), I feel strongly you will find revelation and help in these words regardless of your spiritual beliefs.

As I stated in the beginning of this book, my journey needs to be told not only in the hopes more public awareness of this devastating disorder will bring about healing, but also because what happened to me, from the day I learned the truth of who I was until now is a complete *transformation*.

Moreover, if I can be transformed after being stuck in the torment of abuse for three decades, I feel confident you or your loved one can be released and transformed too!

I use the word *transformation,* defined as: a *thorough or dramatic change in form or appearance,* to title this chapter because who I was for the first forty-nine years of my life changed radically, dramatically and changed *quickly* once I awakened and realized the truth of who I'd become. Furthermore, it started from the inside out.

In a very short period, I went from being an extremely emotionally abusive man; a man who had control and manipulation down to an art form. A man who was *never* wrong (well, except maybe in poker), a man who need not apologize for much of anything because in his sickness could always justify *the truth* (his truth). A man who thought he was the *master communicator;* and a man who believed he was intellectually superior to most other beings walking the planet.

I changed to a man who is completely humbled as a man, husband and father. A man who knows his worth and accomplishments during his abusive years amount to chewed gum on hot asphalt. A man who accepts full responsibility for his actions of the past; a man who *rarely* has angry outburst or abusive tendencies; and a man who for the first time in his life *gets* what it means to be a biblical husband who *lay his life down for his bride*.

In short, for the first time in my life I can say I like who I am! It has taken me 49 years to say that honestly to myself.

Yet unfortunately, even with all the amazing transformations that took place in me over a few short weeks, it still was not enough to change Teri's heart or marriage to me. She simply did not have the will to continue nor did she trust the changes she saw in me were real. She told me "I see the changes but I don't believe or trust them." For her I suppose, seven months of the "new Austin" could not overcome thirty years of the old one.

Yes, over 24 years of marriage I hurt Teri as well as our children. Hurt them bad. I did not fight and leave physical wounds and bruises. No, far worse - I fought with the weapons of the mind. Where I thought I had a distinct advantage and where I knew I could "Win."

Some "Win"...

Upon moving out of our beautiful 2000 sq ft house in the suburbs, I ended up typing most of the journal entries that comprise the core of this book while sitting in my new "home" - a 10'x10' room provided by a friend of mine in the basement of a house he converted into an office

Regardless, I hold out great hope that what I learned on a practical level, and what God revealed to me on a spiritual level, will eventually heal what thirty-years of abuse, manipulation and lies did to Teri and our two daughters.

That is my hope and prayer at least.

our

story

Chapter 2
"I Want a Divorce"

A sound head, an honest heart, and a humble spirit are the three best guides through time and to eternity. That man may safely venture on his way, who is so guided that he cannot stray. _Walter Scott

"I Want a Divorce."

Teri and I had been silent towards each other for the previous two weeks or so which was not unusual in our relationship, but it was normally *me* who initiated the silence. This rather felt different for some reason. Teri was more prone to let everything out, get it over with quickly, to argue, yell, then makeup, and be done with it. The Italian blood in her I suppose.

No, this was different. I could sense it. She's never been the silent type, especially for days on end.

I finally approached her early in the afternoon the 1st of April. She was just getting ready to take a nap or waking up from one— something else she was prone to do when we'd been arguing and felt depressed. I told her she had not said much of anything to me for the past ten days and was wondering if she was going to silence this issue to death. This was my (abusive) way of initiating some discussion.

Allow me to rewind the clock a bit...

Teri mentioned to me one morning she was getting distant from me emotionally, yet didn't want to feel that way. I told her she needed to focus on her relationship with Jesus for a while and forget about the marriage - not in a literal sense but "forget" about the problems we had been having and concentrate more on herself and her relationship with The Lord.

The next morning, as I approached her to say "Good morning" and give her my usual husbandly hug she responded by giving me one of those sideways hugs, reserved for a co-worker, not the normal frontal S Q U E E Z E hug we shared thousands of times over the years.

In my brokenness, I immediately got angry and communicated such by using body and facial expressions without saying a word. That way if needed, I could deny any anger later by saying she must have read my body or facial expressions incorrectly.

Later, Teri came into my office and asked if I was mad. I blurted out without thinking "Not so much mad but there comes a time when the constant ups and downs about how you feel about me becomes not fair to me. I am about ready to call it quits." Ha! This made me the victim and shifted the blame to her.

Lose Teri - win Austin... the kind of fight I honed to razor sharp precision over the past few decades.

She immediately, without saying a word, calmly closed my office door and walked away. Wounded I am sure but hey, at that point it was more about *my* hurt, not hers.

After all, I had been the one who consistently told her how much I loved her, even while enduring all these problems in our relationship and marriage. In addition, I was the one who was "working so hard" on my relationship with Christ, to be a better man and husband of course.

Plus, I was the one who had all the answers, blah, blah, blah. *Stuff a sock in it Skippy!*

I intellectually fought like this for years. Teri always, ALWAYS, came to me and either apologized or initiated some conversation. This behavior let me know my scolding of her had served its purpose, and that it was time to kiss and make up. We would apologize to each other by having great "makeup" sex, and the world would be right again.

Nevertheless, this time she went silent on *me* for the next week and a half. Uh-oh! Houston, we have a problem.

Fast forward back to the 1st of April, the exact conversion is somewhat hazy to me, but I remember the awful highlights.

As she sat up in bed and without the slightest bit of emotion Teri told me she wasn't sure how she felt about me anymore and wasn't sure if she wanted to continue in our marriage. That was about all she needed to say before I took over the conversation.

You see inside I felt threatened by this, scared to death as I look back on it now. Subconsciously, this is what I feared the most during our marriage and why I worked SO HARD to get Teri to a level of total submission and dependence so she could NEVER leave me. Ah, but I jump ahead in the story, sorry.

No, never had Teri so calmly told me her feelings — on the subject of divorce, and I could sense the underlying resolve in what she said. I had to do something to deflect the conversation and find a way to go on the offensive or more precisely, get her on the defensive.

I asked her why stay in the marriage if she did not love me, trying to shift guilt to her. Why stay in something she is not totally committed to I asked. I said something to the effect if she did tell me our marriage was over, it would not affect me much. That I would keep chugging along with my life as if nothing happened.

I -D-I-O-T!

With my words, I *dared* her to say she wanted out. I gave her every reason she needed to tell me it was over.   After all, I told her, this latest attempt to rescue our marriage had been going on for over a year and a half and it obviously wasn't working. It's as if my mouth had taken on a life of its own, blurting out things that though my mind *may* have thought, would never coerce my mouth to say.

The unusual and out of character silence from Teri the past ten days, signaling far in advance that something was majorly wrong, ceased to register as my mouth continued to spew out challenges to Teri.

Teri called my bluff. After I spewed until my 'spewer' was dry, she looked me straight in the eyes and said, "I want a divorce."

"Back at ya Austin." [my words, not hers].

Once the shock of hearing those words set in, and knowing she was serious, the anger wasn't far behind. Anger was always my friend and constant companion for as long as I can remember in this relationship. It was always my ace-in-the-hole, my *go to* weapon of choice when I need a *win*. Yep, with anger by my side, I could always pull out of just about any situation I'd gotten myself into with my wife and, if I was lucky, make it appear as if it was *her* fault.

However, this time the anger trump card didn't work. Nope. Teri calmly stuck by what she said and simply brushed off all my attempts to control her using anger.

With those words - "I want a divorce" - the last brick settled in the wall slowly built around Teri's heart —all because of my words and actions over the years. And I was NOT going to get past that brick wall any longer, no matter what.

Consequently, that day began the most painful and yet the most rewarding journey of my life. Never again do I want to experience the pain of divorce I have experienced - even five years later.

There have been days my heart has hurt SO bad I simply did not know how it could continue to beat—nor did I want it to.

Looking back, I am grateful to Teri she had the guts to say those words to me. For it put me on my path to freedom, freedom from the demon of abuse that controlled me nearly my entire life up until that point.

I was about to come face-to-face with the ugly truth of the man I had become in order to transform to the man I am today.

Thank you, Teri.

Chapter 3
My Signs & Symptoms of Emotional Abuse

The guilty mind debases the great image that it wears, and levels us with brutes. __ Havard

My symptoms and patterns of emotional abuse continued over a period of 30-years. It still amazes me how I was so totally blind to the truth of it for so long, but that is the truth. I had NO IDEA I was an abusive husband and father for the entire twenty-four years of my marriage to Teri, nor did I realize it during the five years we dated.

I realize a lot of you after reading what follows will think "No way! You *had* to know you were abusive at times. I mean come on, thirty Y-E-A-R-S!

Nope, I never had a clue.

I knew I had "some issues" with anger but never correlated that to abuse in any way. In fact, in my sick condition, I thought *my* issues were mild in comparison to Teri's, at least as far as our marriage was concerned. I thought if Teri would get HER issues squared away (insecurity, lack of confidence, learning to communicate better) that MY issues would go away.

Do you see the twisted way abuse works? The issues I thought Teri had and needed to 'fix' were mainly caused by me. Yes, of course, she came into our relationship with some issues due to her childhood, but my abuse magnified them a hundred fold at least. Yet the whole time of our marriage, my focus was primarily on her and her problems and away from mine.

The first time I ever heard the word "abuse" come out of Teri's mouth was about two years prior to our divorce. During an argument, she said she was in an abusive marriage. She immediately said "Not physical abuse, but emotional."

I clearly thought she was out of her mind and merely allowed her anger to get the better of her words. I had no clue what she was talking about and shrugged it off as Teri trying to hurt me during the heat of the moment. Who me, abusive, no way—I love this woman.

With a lemony look on my face, I quickly responded, "What are you *talking* about?" As Teri tried to explain, my twisted mind could only use as a reference her mom's pattern of emotional abuse I witnessed during her interactions with Teri and the periods of abuse Teri shared with me about her childhood. There was *no way* I was like her mom!

After her explanation and in my anger (Gosh, how many days of my life did I spend angry?), I told Teri to list out all the ways I was abusive to her. Less than a minute later, as I stood there seething, I had my list. I don't remember much of what was on it, but I do remember spending the rest of the evening countering each item of *abuse* with my own item of *love, respect* or *caring*.

Never for a second did I stop and wonder if anything on her list was true. Never once did I get the focus off *my* love for Teri and question myself why Teri would come up such a list.

The next day with a scowl on my face I gave her the list she gave me, along with my own, and said something to the effect of how wrong she was and how *my* list proved it.

Folks, the blinders were fully closed over my eyes as to the truth of my abuse and Teri's attempts at waking me up to that truth, did not have *any* impact on me.

The truth is, of course Teri WAS in an emotionally abusive marriage and the abuse started from almost the first time we met.

Though, as I said, I don't remember what Teri put on her list that day, I am confident most all of the behaviors and tendencies I'll share below were on it. What you will read are the main ones that afflicted or controlled me, but keep in mind, there were many other forms of emotional abuse that were more subtle but were just as damaging to Teri and our relationship such as:

- Lying

- Controlling conversations

- Being judgmental, disrespectful, or rude

- Making condescending and patronizing statements

- Withholding affection

- Ignoring promises made

- Betraying her trust in me

Any repeated behavior pattern, be it the more overt ones listed below or the less obvious ones above, are clear warning signs of abusive behavior and should *not* be ignored. They will *not* go away on their own. They cannot because there are *deeply rooted* psychological issues in the individual's mind that needs addressed.

Scientific studies of the brain have proven that our habitual tendencies and thought patterns cut neurotransmitter grooves, or tiny paths into our brain. The brain must be rewired, or new paths through the brain created, in order for a person with such destructive patterns to return to a healthy state of mind. This rewiring is entirely possible, I'm living proof of that, but it is not without a lot of effort and a lot of time.

Think of it as we are in the woods walking along a clear path through the brush and trees, life is good and the walking is easy. Now imagine we must clear a new path through the overgrown brush and thick woods – life is not so easy now. With lots of hard work, persistence and many stops and starts along the way, a new path slowly emerges until one day, we find the walking is easy again. That is what must be done to cut new pathways in our brain.

I cannot stress enough to not fall into the trap of believing that you can change the other person or that with enough love or changes on your part, things will get better. They will not. More than likely YOU will be the one who subtly changes and accepts your mate's behavior, and will find yourself being sucked further and further down into the quicksand of abuse.

Anger

While Teri and I were dating, it didn't take me long to discover I could get just about anything I wanted if I got mad or even upset at Teri. And me getting mad allowed me to get what I wanted most times and that's all that mattered

Though I never thought my anger was an issue – I reasoned it was more like a character flaw - I realize now that over the years, I fed and nurtured my anger monster to the point it slowly became its own entity and took on a life of its own. It became my demon whose sole mission was to destroy my family and me.

It was a subtle progression and I cannot really place a time during the 30-years when it happened, but within a few years, anger consumed and controlled me. Anger became my identity in many ways, all the while fooling me into thinking it was nothing more than a character flaw that I could control if I really wanted to.

I constantly had to *amp up* my anger response to get what I wanted, because Teri would condition herself to my current level, and sometimes not back down and give in as I anticipated.

This did not happen on a conscious level most times, but as my inner-child (more on that later), became more and more fearful, powerless, and insecure of my outside surroundings, I had to stay in control. As I grew older and began to take on more responsibilities as an *adult*, I had to do whatever it took to maintain that control while wearing an 'all is well with me' mask in order to hide those insecurities and fears within me.

Using varying levels of anger allowed me to do just that. I'm sure Teri has a better sense of its progression but I never really gave it a second thought as to how much it started to control *me*.

By using anger all through our dating phase and our entire marriage, I normally ended up the 'victor' of arguments and got just about anything I wanted. All the while not having a clue what it was doing to Teri and our marriage. To Teri, it was easier to give in and let me do, say, or have what I wanted rather than go through the pain of another argument.

I saw some of the effects in Teri – low self-esteem, a willingness to apologize whether she was wrong or not, a propensity to always say "Yes" to me. However, in my twisted mind, those were *her* weaknesses to deal with and certainly not the result of *me* emotionally crippling her.

Yes, anger soon became a daily pattern in my life. Honestly, as I look back now, I probably found something or someone to be angry at just about every day of my life. I was an angry person around the home and around those closest to me.

The standing phrase between my children and Teri around the house was "Is Dad mad?" or "Why is Dad mad?" Instead of compassion when I heard that phrase, I got angry about it. I was completely blinded to my brokenness and the effects that brokenness had on my wife and children.

The underlying "vibe" that permeated through our home all those years was very oppressive with me around. The kids and Teri would constantly walk on eggshells, wondering what kind of mood I was in that day, or even that hour. One minute I would be joking and carrying on yet with a single look or word spoken could be *set off* into a tirade.

Yet outside the home, I was the nicest guy you would ever want to meet. Most abuser's are. It's the Jekyll-Hyde syndrome (more below) and a clear indicator of abuse. I was a manic (bi-polar) mess headed for a train wreck. Up one minute down the next - all the while fooling myself into thinking I was the model of a husband and father.

Yeah, some model.

Expectations

I suppose if there is one underlying *current* or *vibe* that was always flowing through my mind; one thing that was a constant spark that ignited my anger, in most cases, was expectations. As far back as I can remember, even my teenage years while enlisted in the Army, I always had expectations. If I'm being completely transparent, having expectations is something I battle to this day.

On the surface, there is nothing wrong with having expectations, *realistic* expectations, but I had expectations in my head for the way other people should react, how they should think, what they should do, the way they should treat me, and the way they should respond to things that I did or said to them. I had expectations of everyone and expectations for everything in my life!

I kept those expectations to myself, very rarely verbalizing to my family or anyone else what I expected of them, but always keeping score. It is as if I had this score sheet locked in my head, continually grading others based on my expectations. I would then get upset when they did not measure up to what I thought they should do.

In dealing with my family, the times when I didn't get angry, I would nitpick by making suggestions on how they could do things better or how they could have said something different to improve on whatever result I thought they should have.

Let me give an example....

If Teri offered to call a company, concerning a bill we received and then after the call came to me to explain how the conversation went, I would quiz her by saying "Did you ask them about so-and-so?", "Did you think to say this?", or "Did you mention this item on the bill to them?" I would run through my list of expectations that I had for her to cover on the call but I would not discuss those expectations with her BEFORE the call.

In this instance, I might not get angry at her but my voice or facial features, or what I said to her, would clearly express either displeasure or an overwhelming sense that she did not handle the call correctly according to my standards and expectations.

Then, being the great communicator I thought I was, I would say something uplifting like "great job though" to her, after spending the last several minutes expressing my displeasure. This was my abusive, subconscious attempt to always keep Teri off balance and keep her questioning herself, and I thought, keeping her dependent on me.

Another example might be if Teri and the kids decided to clear out part of the garage as a favor to me. I would be very appreciative of what they were doing and would express my pleasure quite openly, but at some point during the clean up, I would go out to the garage and notice some way they could have better organized, or notice some way they could have done things more efficiently, then I would say something to them.

Instead of just letting them clean the cotton-pickin' garage in whatever manner they chose to, and be appreciative of it, I had to open my big mouth and make suggestions of how they could do it better. Of course, all the while thinking in my own head what a great guy I was for helping them be better people while they were helping me.

[*As I type these words, I'm shaking my head back and forth with total disbelief of what an idiot I was. I think of how blinded to the truth I was and how my constant underlying tone of disapproval must have damaged those I love most*]

In looking back, the thoughts and feelings of expectations never seemed to leave my head – they were always there. No matter what I was doing, no matter whom I was with, no matter what situation I was in.

It could be at home, at the workplace; I could be having idle conversation with a friend or an acquaintance. Heck, I could be by myself - I had high expectations of *me* and I very rarely lived up to them. I suppose those failure messages to myself were a result of never measuring up in my mother's eyes after her husband (my dad) died (more on that later).

It was a never-ending cycle for me: 1) have expectations, 2) don't verbalize those expectations, and 3) be upset when those expectations were not met —expectations I never let them know I had! Expectations trapped me in an almost daily pattern of getting angry about something or someone.

Over the years Teri would tell me she felt like she always had to walk on eggshells and I know a big part of the reason why was because there was this underlying feeling in her head that she couldn't live up to my expectations, and she was right.

As I said, I still battle with having expectations to this day. There is a fine, gray line between having healthy expectations and having unhealthy ones. Healthy expectations could be something as simple as expecting someone to return your phone call when they say they will or timely repayment of a debt owed.

But having expectation as to *when* that phone call should be returned or debt paid, and NOT expressing those expectations beforehand, is not healthy and is a slippery slope I traverse from time to time.

I am a work in progress, will be 'til the day I die —I suppose.

Silence

I also found out early in our relationship that if I went silent for a period during or after an argument, I could really *get back* at Teri. Since this was always done in response to her hurting ME, I thought I was totally justified. After all, *all is fair in love and war*, right?

I remember reading "*Men Are From Mars, Women Are From Venus*" and the author, John Gray, talking about men and their *caves*. He wrote men just naturally need their *alone time,* in their cave, to decompress, think, cool down or do whatever else men do while in their caves.

This cave didn't need to be a physical location (though it could), but may involve sitting in the lazy-boy recliner flipping through channels on the remote or reading the newspaper. Mr. Gray specifically said while the men are in their caves, they are to be left alone and if the woman dares to come in, it is *her* own fault if the dragon (the cave dragon I guess) slays her.

I took the *cave thing* to the extreme of course, all in an attempt to justify my actions or to manipulate results, or both.

Depending on the level of *hurt* I was experiencing, I would go to my cave anywhere from hours to days, sometimes even a week, or more! I would go days and days without saying a word to Teri, literally not one word - hurtful glares yes, words no. I became a master of manipulation, making everything look like somehow it was all her fault and I was the victim, no matter what the issue was. All I to do was sulk enough around the house.

After a while, the silence would get to Teri and she would try to approach me in an effort to end the silent treatment and reconcile, but I did not see it that way. In my mind, she entered my cave and I had every right to lash out at her in whatever method I deemed appropriate, but the reality was, it was my attempt to always be the one in control - I had to be the one to determine when it was time to kiss and makeup, not Teri.

A man's cave was never meant to be used as a weapon but I was a master at it. I could stew for days or weeks on end and allow all the injustices Teri *ever* committed against me to bounce around in my head like a pinball—with the Pinball Wizard mashing the flippers!

My thoughts consumed and controlled me. At times, I would rage at her inside my mind, sometimes completely forgetting what started the initial disagreement or what the core issue involved. It did not matter. I was *mad* at her!

I know now this literally ate Teri up inside and crushed her spirit. Here God gave me this precious flower as a wife, to tend to and nurture, and I chose to simply lay that beautiful flower under my feet and crush it—all because *I could*.

Never once did I have the thought that this was abuse. In some sick, twisted way, I thought this kind of behavior between a husband and wife was *normal*. The fighting was ugly but as long as the *other times* were fine (according to my expectations), everything was okay. After all, we loved each other.

In the latter years of our marriage, as I would be in my cave mentally rehashing *stuff* from years ago, I started to ask myself *why I am acting this way.* I didn't *want* to be mad at Teri, I didn't want to be mad at anyone, but it was if I could not help it. I hated that I was acting this way but could not control or stop it.

I would tell myself *STOP IT!* However, I could not listen. The more I tried to control the rage the madder I would become and generally, that anger would manifest itself towards others.

Of course, trying to stop my anger was my own internal warning mechanisms trying to get my attention, but I was too far gone to realize it or do much to stop it.

The train wreck was getting closer and closer and in my brokenness, I could do nothing to stop it. I didn't have a clue what the underlying problems in my life were, nor did I spend even one minute trying to figure them out.

A demon controlled me—I was a merely a puppet to its control and manipulation. I know those times of questioning and trying to stop myself were an inner cry for help. Yet I didn't know enough or in my pride wouldn't allow myself to reach out for the help I desperately needed. I was still completely oblivious to how utterly broken I was and how desperately I needed help.

My pride wouldn't allow me to go to Teri when all had blown over and humbly tell her the torment I battled in my mind. That it was NOT the person I wanted to be and needed help. No, I would shrug it all off once things between Teri and I was back to "normal, " and simply go on with life. Enjoy the good times now that the bad times were behind us. It is commonly called the honeymoon phase in the three cycles of abuse: honeymoon - escalation - explosion.

Nevertheless, for the victims of abuse, it is not quite so easy to compartmentalize those events and give it the ole "Que Sera Sera"* (kay sa-rah sa-rah) and move on. The deep emotional wounds of abuse are not so easily healed.

For those too young to remember, Que Sera Sera is a song made popular by Doris Day in a movie.

Once, Teri shared with me that growing up her brother would go to his room and stay there most of the time, never socializing with the family and usually eating in his room, watching television, separated from everyone else. Teri would knock on his door and ask why he would not talk to her or anyone else in the family but he wouldn't answer.

It hurt Teri because she thought that somehow it was her fault. Silence was a way to punish in Teri's household and I learned early how to use this to my advantage too.

Still, none of what I classified as *character flaws*, my inner cries for help, or my issues with anger was evident to me as emotional abuse. I guess because of Teri's brokenness growing up in an abusive home, perhaps for a while, this all seemed *normal* to her too (just part of the ups and downs of marriage).

Man do I wish someone, anyone, would of taken me behind the wood shed and whipped my butt, HARD, after witnessing the way I treated my wife. Maybe I would have awakened before it was too late.

Codependency and the Rescuer

Because of Teri's upbringing, she came into our marriage codependent on me. In general terms, someone codependent is relying on someone else for his or her happiness. Their thinking and focus centers around that other person and they begin to react to that person's external cues rather than their own internal cues.

Truth be told, I think most people enter into a relationship as codependent in some way, expecting the other person to provide their happiness or to subconsciously heal psychological wounds from their past.

Too many people marry someone because of what they think they are going to get out of the relationship rather than what they can put into the relationship. Too many times, they go by how the other person *makes them feel* rather than evaluating whether there is a good match on a more intimate level.

Nothing wrong with feelings mind you, it is just a lousy way to evaluate something as important as the lifelong commitment that marriage intends to be. Eventually those feelings will come under fire and be strenuously tested in the marriage, and far too often people decide to bail on the current relationship and look for those feelings with someone else.

As our marriage progressed, I slowly became (what is known as), a *rescuer*. We'd all like to think of ourselves as someone who would go out of their way to help rescue an injured animal or a bird with a broken wing, right? A rescuer in a relationship feels they need to help the other person who is somehow injured.

They take on the role of trying to fix someone when in reality none of us can fix another person; we can only fix ourselves and love the other person as they work on fixing themselves.

In a healthy relationship both people need to always be looking for ways to help their mate of course, we are to give more than receive, yes. Nevertheless, there is a balance to the giving. When one begins to think they are more responsible for the other person than the other person does (talking adult relationships here), it becomes an unhealthy relationship for sure.

I somehow felt responsible for Teri.   She was that bird with a broken wing and due to my sorrow over her upbringing, I somehow felt responsible for fixing her—I was the one to make Teri *healthy*. I felt responsible to step in and protect her, educate her, and do things for her. After all, I was the man; the protector and provider and head of the family. It was my job was it not?

All the while, I was psychologically broken tremendously but somehow managed to give the persona that I could handle any situation that came along and Teri seemed to acquiesce to my macho image and persona.

This served to make Teri more codependent on me and in turn allowed me to transition my love for her into a 24/7 pattern of control, manipulation, and emotional abuse.

Looking back, I felt I was somehow responsible for Teri being a better person than she was. That somehow it was my job to make her better.

I don't know why I didn't think Teri was great just the way she was (she was and still is!), but I felt she could be *better* and as the man, *the rescuer*, it was all up to me to show her how. I felt it my duty, as her loving husband, to help her whether she asked for it or not.

Over the years, I would constantly question her decisions. Mind you, not in cruel or undermining ways but rather with a "Are you sure?" bias to them. I did this because I thought I knew what was best for Teri in many situations, and as the rescuer, felt I needed to 'guide' her along the way. In my deceived mind, I thought I was being a good husband and helping her, but, on my abusive side, the intellectual way I would go about it naturally made Teri question whether her decisions were the right ones to make.

Many times Teri would say she was going to do something a certain way but it would be stated to me in the form of a question, so naturally I needed to add my opinion to the mix in order to improve *her* outcome.

This quickly served to be very emotionally abusive to Teri because she was always second-guessing her decisions. She was always questioning if what she was doing was the right thing or not – it was always according to *my standards* that she would be second guessing herself, not her own standards or internal cues. My standards were Teri's external cues that she relied on, rather than relying on her intuition as to whether her decision was the correct one or not.

Instead of lifting her up, it only served to knock her down. That is the exact intent of a chronic emotional abuser; push the other person down until they are completely dependent.

This *dependence* served two purposes for me: subconsciously I thought if I made Teri completely dependent on me she could never leave me. Through my control of her, I did not have to face my inner fears, my inner child, who was scared to death to be operating in the world where it operated.

I was emotionally locked and only capable of processing my world through the eyes of a twelve or thirteen year old, not a man who was in his twenties and thirties (I'll discuss this *emotional lock* later on).

All throughout my marriage, I thought Teri was the one making most of the mistakes and therefore needed most of the correcting. I thought I was normally right about things and therefore needed to be the one to make most (all?) the major decisions in our marriage. Moreover, it was somehow up to me, as I stated before, to *correct* Teri so she could became the woman that I'm sure she wanted to be.

Here is an example of how emotionally unstable I was becoming and how blind to it all I was. Remember the song that came out in the 80's by Bette Midler - Wind Beneath My Wings? It contained the words "Did I ever tell you you were my hero?" I can remember for years after that song came out, thinking that would probably be the song Teri would sing or dedicate to me because surely, I must be her hero; that I was the wind beneath her wings!

What with everything I did for her and all the great decisions I made along the way and how she could depend on me in any situation to take charge and be the man of the family and how I was helping her be a better person (yadda yadda yadda).

What a bunch of bunk!

I was incapable of rescuing myself much less rescuing anyone else, yet it was a role I took on and Teri, due to her own abusive upbringing, allowed me to resume.

Control

My need to be in control of every facet of my life stemmed from an underlying issue of low self-esteem and as I mentioned above, my mind being locked emotionally to that of a young child due to events surrounding my Dad's death (Neither of these issues would be revealed to me until much later in my life however). My father died when I was fifteen and I don't think I ever fully recovered from his death until I broke free from my abuse, thirty-three after he died.

Soon after graduating high school, I joined the Army. I came home after four years full of self confidence (so I thought) and a *can do* attitude in just about everything I faced, but inside I was a deeply trouble young man. However, taking charge of situations was something ingrained deep within me during my four years in the military, so I was not afraid to take charge and make decisions upon transitioning back to "The world." Two years after my discharge, Teri and I were married.

Teri's codependency combined with my underlying need to be a rescuer, my military *take charge* training, and the psychological wounding I received after my dad died, set our marriage up for failure right from the outset. There was no chance for equality between Teri and I as husband and wife, and though God saw us as "one flesh" in his eyes, there was never an emotional bond that formed between us.

In many ways, I thought I was intellectually superior to Teri and perhaps in her brokenness she agreed, at least initially. Not that I didn't think Teri was smart (much smarter than I as it turned out), but I came into the relationship with a *Me Tarzan, You Jane* attitude.

Part of my feeling was out of a sincere interest to take care of and provide for my wife, but it soon morphed into a subconscious feeling of *I'm up here and you're down there,* so just follow what I say and do and everything will be alright. Very rarely was I able to approach our relationship on a level playing ground. I *had* to stay in control in order to protect my inner-child.

Using mostly anger and silence as weapons, I easily took charge of most any situation we faced and after a while, Teri simply acquiesced and let me take control of most of the decision-making. After all, it was going to end up with things being done my way so why fight it? Oh sure, I'd always ask her opinion on things and we would sit down and discuss important situations before going forward but I'll bet if a tally was kept, 90% or more of the time things where done the way I wanted them done.

Control in itself isn't a bad thing. We all need some level of control to function normally in life and for most of us; not being in control is somewhat of a scary thing. However, in the hands of a sick, abusive mind like mine, control was down to a level of the Nth degree. I mean, I believed the dishwasher needed to be loaded a certain way because any other way wasn't as efficient.

Let me list some of the control issues I had that quickly come to mind:

- Very rarely did I support Teri's decisions or the things she wanted to do

- Very rarely did I get involved with her hobbies yet I always wanted her to be involved with mine if for no other reason than spending time together

- As for the way she dressed? Well, I knew the way she looked best; I would buy her the clothes I wanted her to wear

- I handled the checkbook, paid the bills, and calculated our budget

- Most times I determined the type of sex we'd have

- Decided where we'd go out to eat, what movies to watch

- I thought I could read Teri's mind and that I knew her better than she knew herself.

The list goes on and on over a 30-year relationship but the bottom line was, I *always* had to have things *my* way.

I think the only two areas that I didn't absolutely try and control Teri was in the job she had and whether she wore her hair long or short (she looks cute either way).

Control freak doesn't begin to describe it folks. However, at no time did I ever think my level of control was *out of control*.

Manipulation

If I was *good* at other forms of abuse and control I have mentioned, I was a PhD, fully certified, Master-Ninja EXPERT in manipulation. In my need to control, I learned quickly how to subtly impose my will on Teri and those around me. I don't know when I became so good at it, but I could twist words, juggle conversations, ask leading questions, impart guilt, withhold affection, throw facial or body expressions, use hostile humor, and outright beg if all else failed in order to maneuver situations and control outcomes.

On the outside, I was a man, but inside I was a scared little boy. Mind games became second nature to me in order to survive in the big bad world.

Manipulation is a terribly effective weapon because it is crafted and used in such sneaky ways that many times the one manipulated begins to accept their mind being controlled as normal; it just becomes an ordinary part of their life.

It is very hard to define an art. I mean, how would you describe, in detail, how to paint a portrait or a landscape? Can you describe how to photograph the very best picture you ever took? It is very difficult.

You can speak of generalities of course, but the specific strokes and nuances of the craft are very difficult to describe on paper. With that, it's hard for me to give specific examples of exactly how and when I manipulated, especially after almost five years of freedom from it.

However, with the aid of material from a class I took, I will give the broad-brush strokes of the type of manipulation I used to great effect and with it, perhaps you will recognize a pattern of behavior in your own situation. This is just a fragment of the tools of manipulation I used over the decades.

Never accepting blame or responsibility

For years, I would ask Teri to be honest with me and share her feelings about situations or simply in our day-to-day married life. Yet, many times when she *was* honest and perhaps pointing out my shortcoming, I would twist the conversation so I did not have to accept any blame or be responsible for upsetting her.

Say for instance I forgot to pay a pay a bill on time and Teri brought it to my attention in a gentle manner; perhaps as simple as asking, "Did you pay the electric bill this month?" I would immediately say something like "No, I've been so busy at work the last few weeks I completely forgot. I wish you would've reminded me a few days ago." It was obviously my responsibility to get the bill paid on time, but I subtly shift the blame to Teri because she did not remind me when I thought she should of.

Saying one thing but denying it later

I was an expert at denying the things I knew I had said in previous conversations, or just a few minutes ago. I could justify, rationalize, turn earlier statements around, or explain why what I *really* said was not at all, what it sounded like I said. I could explain what I said wasn't what I meant, or if all else failed, I'd flat out lie, all the while wrapping my words in such a persuasive argument I'm sure Teri had to start questioning her own sanity or her ability to remember our conversations. I simply would not be denied most times manipulating the 'truth' to what I desired it to be.

Laying guilt

Due to Teri's childhood, she was always one to assume a fair amount of guilt in just about any interaction we had, whether it was warranted or not (most times it was not). I used this to my advantage whenever the mood struck me and since I was someone who could not take responsibility for my own actions or shortcomings, the mood struck me quite often.

I could make Teri feel guilty for speaking her mind or not speaking it; for being emotional or not being emotional enough; for giving and caring, or for not giving and caring enough. Anything was fair game with me. Even the times when Teri was right about something during a discussion or argument we were having, I would often send her away feeling guilty for being right—for hurting *my* feelings in the process.

Never accepting "No" for an answer

I could not accept "No" for an answer on things I wanted. I would constantly re-approach, coming from a new angle each time, until Teri relented and gave in to my ceaseless (and mostly senseless) requests. Two specific examples come to mind.

I wanted a second dog and Teri didn't think it was such a good idea. Back and forth, we went for days. I would show her pictures of puppies to win her over. I would say in a joking (but I was serious) manner how much our other dog would love the companionship. I constantly researched breeders and prices online and shared my findings with Teri.

During dinners, I would make some type of *wanting another dog* comment and then display my best pouting face because I was so sad not to have one. It got so bad I eventually got on my hands and knees one evening and begged Teri, in a half-joking, laughing (but, oh so serious) kind of way until she finally wore down and relented.

I *would not* stop until I got my way because in my mind, her reasons for not getting another dog were not really very good. Not sure what ever happened to "No, I really don't think it's a good idea" reason being a good enough all on its own.

Another time, after moving to a new town, I wanted a new boat. I should point out that many times my "wants" were spur of the moment, out of left field desires. Teri thought financially it wasn't the right time for us to make a major purchase. On and on I went about how we could afford it. I would bring up all the fun we had when we co-owned a boat previously with her parents and how much fun the kids would have.

I took her to a boat show, "just looking" of course. I used every tactic I could think of to get that stupid boat to the point we would argue about it and I would attempt to lay a guilt trip on her because she was denying me. Of course, I eventually wore her down and again, she gave in.

The two best days I had with that boat were the day we bought it and the day we sold it. Never did it bring me the happiness I thought it would, nor was it worth the price I made Teri pay emotionally to get it.

Looking back, I think the bigger "thrill" was simply getting my way. It was like some kind of adrenaline rush just to figure out a new way to approach her, a new tactic to use on her, figure out some way to get her to *agree with me* that doing or buying whatever I wanted was the best way to go.

It was not the 'stuff' that brought me happiness. It was the rush of being able to manipulate in order to get what I wanted that was the prize.

Another similar tactic I used to get what I wanted was to initially ask for something that was clearly unreasonable, which I knew (and expected) would get a "No" answer. Say for instance expressing an interest in taking flying lessons. I (rightly) knew that Terri would respond with a negative answer, and then I would come back with a much *smaller* request like purchasing a radio-controlled airplane.

I would drag Teri along to the hobby store "just to show her what I was talking about," and then would go on and on about how I wanted it with the salesman and with Teri standing nearby. Her guilt at saying no to the flying lessons would cause her to say "Yes" to my *new hobby.* She knew from experience that I would not let up until she agreed to let me do whatever I wanted to do.

Here is the topper: If during any future discussion or argument Teri brought up a purchase I made, and she mentioned it was a bad decision, or mentioned it caused financial hardship for us, in my sickness I couldn't accept the blame, I'd come back with something like "Well, you should of put your foot down and not allowed me to buy it."

Yeah, right.

Using others to get what I wanted

I was not beyond using friends or sometimes even the kids to get what I wanted or get a message to Teri if I thought I could manipulate a situation to get my way. I would talk to a mutual friend about an issue, hoping she would eventually get into a discussion with Teri and mention what I had said. All this was done in such a subtle manner that the friend wouldn't know I was playing her against Teri.

I could probably go on and think of a few more examples of my manipulation but frankly, I'm getting sick to my stomach in reliving the few examples I've detailed already.

I told you in the opening of this book I would reveal the *ugly truth* about the awful monster I was for 3 decades. If there is anything positive gleaned from what I have written so far, 95% of these abusive tendencies are completely gone in me today, and the 5% that remain do not control me anymore. They resurface in my mind occasionally, but I treat them as a reminder that I still have a ways to go in my recovery, or perhaps they are a reminder of who I was, or what I had become. It keeps me a humbled man, especially to those whom I hurt.

Rejecting Authority

I hated authority all the years I was abusive. I simply could not allow anyone or anything tell me what to do. I don't think I held down a job for more than five years at a stretch. Although I must add that since I was in the IT field, it wasn't unusual to jump jobs in order to get healthy pay raises each time.

I did manage to increase my salary quite a bit during our marriage but I *always* had a boss who was *a jerk* in my opinion and could always give specific examples as to why.

At times, my disdain for authority at the workplace would get so bad that I would fly off the deep end and find some home-based business that held the answer to all our financial issues (that I caused) as well as an answer for me working for idiots. Instead of working on the business part-time while still holding down my full time job, I would announce I was quitting my job—after getting *approval* from Teri of course.

Never once did those businesses pan out, so back to the corporate world I would go. Luckily, I always seemed to land a well-paying job, but the reality was I put our finances so far behind while working on some cock-a-mammy business idea that we were always behind financially. More importantly, I was robbing Teri of the stability she so desperately needed in her life.

Most married women (generalizing of course) have a *deep need* to have stability—stability in their relationships, in their home, and in their finances. Because of all my job changes—going from a job to my own business back to a job—and all the financial pressures those changes brought with them, Teri was constantly under tremendous stress—she had no stability!

Of course it was all about me, and I always justified what I was doing by saying I was merely trying to be a good provider for the family (and there were times when I was). However, even if Teri had approached me about how she felt I would have somehow twisted it around to make it look like she was not supporting *our financial future and me*. I would convince her she was not being a good wife.

My need to escape from under an authoritative corporate environment caused our financial stability to suffer but I had trouble dealing with authority on all levels. I could not stand for someone to tell me what to do, if it prevented me from doing what I wanted to do.

Hostile Humor

I would venture to guess most people use this form of abusive communication in one way or another from time to time. How many times have we been in a public situation with a person we are a little 'miffed' at for some reason, and an opportunity comes along to say something to them directly or about them to someone else, said in a "totally joking manner," that ends up being a put down or insult or something negative about them?

Of course it is all done *in fun*, or so we say, but the underlying 'gotcha' message is there, and it's all because we are still upset in some way over an argument we had with them or something they did or said to upset us in the past.

Have you ever made *joking* comments to someone else about your wife's cooking or how well the other person keeps their home while your wife is present (hoping your wife will get the clue)? Ever joked with your mutual friends, while your husband is close by, about the way he doesn't pay the bills on time or is constantly late for events that are important to you, or he forgot about your anniversary last month?

Of course, you are *over it* but the temptation of getting that *dig* in was too overwhelming to let it pass by.

These are all examples of hostile humor. A way to *get even*, or get your point across, or attempt to manipulate someone, all the while wrapping the statements around some form of humor or laughing and acting as if you're 'just kidding' with the person. Could be spoken directly to that person or could be spoken to someone else but certainly directed at the other person.

Anytime you say something using a joking tone or laugh, which has a direct underlying message to someone else, it's considered hostile humor —it degrades the other person.

I had no idea how much hostile humor goes on between couples or even friends until I began to study it as part of my recovery. It is a nasty form of projecting anger, control, or manipulation on someone and it is something I used thousands of times against Teri in an effort to make additional *jabs* at her if I felt I was hurt or wounded from a previous discussion, or I was attempting to lay guilt on her after the fact.

I always said the statements with a laugh or chuckle or in a jokingly enough manner that later, if she brought it to my attention, I could defend my actions and say to her "I was just kidding. My, where's your sense of humor?" and follow up with she needed to lighten up or not let her guilty conscious affect her so much.

It's part of the multitude of tools an abusive person uses to *always* keep their victims off balance or second guessing themselves, in an attempt to keep the blame and focus off of themselves and their immaturity.

I was a master at it—ALL of it.

Jekyll-Hyde Personality

Towards the latter stages of our marriage, Teri would occasionally blurt out I had a Jekyll-Hyde personality or tell me I was 'manic', 'bi-polar', or "always up or down." I thought she was nuts. I had a constant barrage of excuses and rational explanations for my behavior: I was a very passionate person, I had emotions just like everyone else, I wore my heart on my sleeve and therefore my feelings could be hurt easily, or I just happen to be having a bad day. "Why aren't I allowed to be emotional and have varying feelings just like everyone else?" I would ask her.

I think I looked up bi-polar a few times on the Internet but that was more because I didn't really know what the word meant rather than thinking for a second I suffered from it. My moods were up, down or sideways... and dramatic most times. I could change in an instant depending on what someone said to me, or how they looked at me, or if I wasn't getting my way.

Of course, I did have a Jekyll-Hyde personality but I was too blind to see it. Outside the home, I came across as the nicest guy you would ever want to meet - charming, personable, funny, and honest. Nevertheless, inside the home I could morph into the exact opposite of that persona in an instant.

Teri and the kids were living with two different people - Dr. Jekyll and Mr. Hyde - and they NEVER knew which one was going to be present from one minute to the next. They constantly walked on eggshells for fear Mr. Hyde would make his appearance at the drop of a hat.

Jekyll-Hyde Syndrome is a form of personality disorder known as Borderline Personality Disorder (BPD). The American Psychiatric Association list 257 different manifestations of BPD and estimates over eighteen million people suffer from the disorder!

Discussing Jekyll-Hyde or BPD in any type of detail is way beyond the scope of this book. I'm certainly nowhere near competent enough to lay at all the nuances of such a complex disorder, but I can discuss my experiences with it and some common signs that you can look for in yourself or your partner.

Adults who suffer from the Jekyll-Hyde personality are normally always emotionally undeveloped due to some type of childhood trauma that prevented their normal emotional growth from taking place. On the outside, a Jekyll-Hyde is in an adult body, but on the inside they think, feel, act, and react as a child and the age of the child depends on the age of their childhood trauma.

The Jekyll Hyde personality normally manifest during a stressful time. I would have quick and extreme mood swings because the child in me could not handle or regulate the emotions I was feeling—rejection, fear, loss of control, etc. I handled those feelings just as any young child would by lashing out in anger and saying things that hurt the other person; I would throw a good old-fashioned temper tantrum and do or say anything I could to try and get my way.

I mentioned before having unrealistic expectations of people in general and Teri specifically. This is a classic symptom of the Jekyll-Hyde personality. Early in our relationship, I placed Teri up on a pedestal and in my mind created very high and unrealistic expectations for her—how I felt she was to treat and act towards me.

Because I was a child inside, it was important for me to get my security from Teri so that I knew "my world" would be okay. Once I realized she was not living up to those expectations (no one can live up to the expectations a Jekyll-Hyde has for them), I began to degrade her and put her down.

If you have young children, think how they look towards you for their entire sustenance and security. YOU are their rock and as long as they know you will be there for them they are okay, and they can handle life and their surroundings.

That was the same subconscious feeling I had toward Teri, but no person can stand up under that type of god-ship. A parent can and does fulfill that role for a brief time in a child's life, but a good parent is constantly pushing a child to become self-sufficient and not dependent on them as a parent as they get older.

A healthy adult relationship has no room for one person to expect the other to provide their security, happiness, and well-being. Yet inside I was not an adult, I was still a little child.

As was the case with me, most individuals affected by BPD often exhibit a fear of abandonment. Although I never had issues with Teri going for a *girl's night out* or even a *girl's only* vacation, my underlying, subconscious fear was of her leaving our relationship and me.

The way I reacted upon that fear, using control, manipulation, and abuse, was defeating the very relationship I was scared to lose. People caught in Jekyll-Hyde relationships have a very difficult time getting their marriage to mature into a deeper level of intimacy and bonding, or moving into a deeper level of trust—all of which are essential for a healthy, mature marriage.

As I mentioned earlier, my behavior caused Teri and the kids to walk on eggshells much of the time they were around me. At times, they could sense an underlying vibe of stress in the house and they constantly wondered if I was going to change into Mr. Hyde at a moment's notice.

In a twist of irony, at my previous job I worked for a man who was emotionally and verbally abusive. It was a small office environment and we could feel the entire vibe of the office change any time this man was around. It was due to us never knowing what kind of mood he would be in or if his mood would suddenly and radically change because someone did or said something to set him off.

Any time he was away from the office for an extended period it was a much more relaxed environment; the office could enjoy the workday free of any underlying stress. Many times It occurred to me while working there that the negative environment at the office was the exact type of environment I projected in my own home towards my family.

Another example of my Jekyll-Hyde personality: I could argue with Teri the entire time we were getting ready for church and during the drive to church. But once out of the car in the parking lot, I would put my 'nice guy' mask on and be an example of the perfect Christian husband and father—greeting and smiling to others, and worshiping the Lord as if nothing was wrong.

Then the mask would come off on the way back home and I would continue the argument or use the silent treatment and not speak a word to her or anyone else for who knows how long.

Most people who knew me fairly well during the 30-years of my abuse couldn't believe it, after I became healthy, when I told them I was an emotionally abusive man, husband, and father. I was very good at wearing different masks and being different people depending on if I was in public or in private.

Criticizing

Me criticizing Teri kind of goes along with the section above on manipulation, I criticized so many times and in so many different ways, it would be impossible for me to recap them all for you now.

As I mentioned above, I looked at myself as a rescuer, my job was to save and help Teri become the woman (I thought) she wanted to be. I reasoned in my own head since she was emotionally, verbally and at times physically abused growing up; she was incapable of growing into that woman on her own.

While Teri and I were divorcing, I asked her if this description was pretty close to what she perceived of my criticism - "In my attempts to make you better, I become overly critical of you all the time." She agreed that was close. As I mentioned I had this subconscious feeling that I was to make Teri better.

I constantly offered suggestions of ways she could be better at whatever it was she was doing—everything from cleaning the house, doing laundry, cooking, grocery shopping or the way she communicated or disciplined the girls. I ALWAYS found something that she did, did not do, or something she could improve on or eliminate to make her a better woman, wife or mother in my opinion.

She might do ninety-nine out of one hundred things correctly but I would normally point out the one thing she would miss. I could give a broad "Good job" compliment on the ninety-nine things she did right, but I might elaborate on the one thing I thought she did wrong.

I never was verbally violent towards Teri by calling her names and certainly never threatened physical violence towards her. Nevertheless, I had this uncanny knack of always being able to keep her off balance; an ability to always make sure she questioned herself or never gained confidence in herself, or gained confidence in her decision making abilities, or confidence in her actions.

It goes hand in hand with the need to control of course but in my mind, I never questioned if what I was doing was wrong. I thought perhaps I was a little extreme at times, but I was never wrong.

Chapter 4
Set Free From my Prison

Let us watch well our beginnings, and results will manage themselves.
__Alex Clark

It was soon after hearing those words of divorce back in April and knowing in my soul our marriage was over that things began to change in me. In the Bible there is a verse that says "Then you will know the truth and the truth will set you free."

Over the next few weeks, the truth about the man I had become was about to be revealed to me.

After Teri told me she wanted a divorce my heart broke. I think the afternoon she told me my abusive side came out and I said one or two things out of anger in a feeble attempt to try to regain control, but by the next day, the reality of the situation hit me.

Despite all the things I did to Teri over the course of our marriage, the fact was, I loved Teri with all my heart—she is the love of my life. I fell for her while I was a senior and she was a sophomore in high school. She was the first and only woman to whom I ever made love. The problem was I never knew HOW to love Teri. We had zero role models on either side of the family in which to base our relationship as a newly married couple.

When Teri and I formed our friendship, my dad had died three years prior from Leukemia and my mom was emotionally whacked out over his death. My dad was mom's sustenance and security and for the next 33 years after his death, she spiraled deeper and deeper into depression.

Teri's dad was battling a lifelong drinking problem and was not around much, even when he was 'around' (he eventually conquered alcoholism and was 12 years sober when he died praise God!), and Teri's mom spent most of life being pissed at Teri's dad and angry at the world. To say we didn't have any role models to pattern our marriage after would be an understatement.

The realities of divorce were not something I grew up with nor was it something accustomed to on my side of the family. On either side of my mom or dad's family only one cousin was divorced, everyone else somehow managed to stay together. When I faced the reality that my marriage was more than likely going to end, it was a shock - 'shock' doesn't really describe the feeling I had but I don't know there's a word that does.

I was totally shaken to the core of my being. Devastated; eviscerated. I had nothing and there was no fight left in me. It was if I lost all reason to fight because fighting would no longer do any good. I still had all the abusive tendencies within me but as I stated before, my underlying reason for the abuse, control, and manipulation was in some sick way to keep Teri dependent on me so she would not leave me.

Teri stating she wanted a divorce was her drawing a line in the sand, and I knew there was not any reason to try and cross it because I also knew she was serious. Finally, after three decades, I gave up the fight.

For days and weeks afterward, I spent hours and hours on the floor crying and crying out to God. Crying because I knew that I failed, that I was a failure, and crying to God for help—I had nowhere else to turn. I didn't know the exact reason why I failed (I still had no clue I was abusive), but I knew that I had. I could not cope with life and since I was not working at the time, spent most of my waking hours bawling uncontrollably.

It was the start of surrendering myself totally and was the key to my recovery. I had reached my breaking point, and as would be revealed to me over the next several weeks, a time of discovering the real me—Mr. Austin "Abuser" James.

As the hidden truth began to find its way into my conscious thoughts, slowly, as molasses pours in the winter air, I became aware that my anger 'issue' was not just an 'issue' at all. No, it was its own entity; one that I invited in as a friend and nurtured, but in a short period of time, it took full control of me.

Me being angry wasn't a character flaw as I brushed it off to be during the early years, it WAS my character; it's who I was identified as being, what I was in one form or another almost every day of my life.

Coming to full grips with this anger inside me, was a tremendous blow to me and a tremendous relief to me all at the same time. It was devastating to know I was an 'angry man' for longer than I could remember. It was devastating to know that my anger not only affected Teri and the kids in a very fearful way for so many years, but that I had allowed anger to control nearly every facet of my life.

Yet at the same time, it was a relief because I *knew* it was a completely separate entity from *who I* was, as a person. Yes, it was the person I had become because at some point in my life, I relinquished control of myself, but it was not the person that was really *me*. It was not Austin James; it was something outside of who the real Austin James was. Moreover, knowing this gave me hope and a confidence that I could get rid of it.

Once I was able to separate the anger entity from myself, I started to take control of the situation and reject every time I had an angry thought or impulse. This did not occur instantaneously, it was only after much prayer and allowing God to show me how to get this *thing* out and away from me.

If I began to have angry thoughts or felt anger starting to well up inside me, and I were in a place where I could talk freely, I would say aloud "No! Get away from me! I do NOT accept you. I am a peaceful man, full of love! I am a Child of God and I bring the name of Jesus against you!"

At first, I was saying this kind of stuff, aloud or within my mind, it seemed, hundreds of times a day—it was a battle. Anger was so much a part of me, deep within my soul, that it wasn't easy getting rid of it.

Sometimes I would go ten or twenty minutes, allowing my anger to take me wherever it wanted to go before I had a conscious realization of what was going on within my mind and remembered I could battle the thoughts.

I became *aware.* Aware of the thoughts that were in my mind whereas all the years before this, I simply allowed my thoughts to take me wherever *they* wanted to go. It's as if I woke up to a new level of consciousness and discovered I was no longer at the mercy of my thoughts; that I had the power and ability to decide if I wanted to hold on to certain ones or reject them.

During this time, I was still completely blind to the fact I was abusive. I was strictly dealing with my anger, but anger was the core underlying problem in me (or so I thought), and was the first thing I needed to address because it was the overwhelming trait that I dealt with on almost a daily basis.

All this took several weeks to fully register and comprehend in my mind. During this time, I was still a basket case and could not go more than a few hours without completely losing it emotionally. I didn't exhibit any anger or abusive behaviors during this time but emotionally, I was wrung-out, drained, and numb.

It was all I could do to make it through the day. I tried to put on a good face for Teri and the kids during this time and had decided not to tell them what I discovered just yet until I had a better grasp of it myself. I am sure my *good face* did not fool them but I did try to appear and act normal—whatever *normal* was at that point in my life.

I especially did not want the kids to constantly see or hear me crying because the level at which I did so was a little alarming. Besides, 'dad crying' was a foreign concept to my children.

The Urge to Purge

When the overwhelming need to cry came over me - *cry* being a vast understatement to the actual process - I would go off by myself, simply wilt to the ground, and bawl. Tears would flow out of me as they have never flowed from me in my life. Someone would exhibit the same grief stricken cry when he or she just found out some loved one unexpectedly died.

I would lay there with my mouth open and ball with absolutely no sound coming out of me, just like a baby does when they've hurt themselves and begin to wail but the 'wail' takes several moments to catch up with the rest of the event.

It was if I was emptying myself of more than just tears - the same type of emptying you might do, not to be gross, when you are sick as a dog leaning over the toilet vomiting. I was not emptying my stomach, I was purging something inside me, but it was the same kind of 'completely drained', not-one-ounce-of-strength-in-my-body weakness.

I started referring to these episodes as 'the urge to purge'. I had no control over when the urge would come upon me nor did I have any control over how long they lasted. All I could do was lay there and let whatever fluids were going to come out of me come out, while I simply tried to gasp for breath in between wailing spasms.

As terrible as those moments were, I began to realize over the coming months that it was my pride, ego, and all sorts of nastiness coming out, and it was a needed process for me to go through.

You cannot rebuild something unless you first completely tear it down and throw away the unwanted trash, and there was a boatload of trash within me.

These episodes would continue for many years into my recovery and still occur occasionally today. I welcome the urge to purge now because I realize God has additional 'junk' in my heart to purge before He can fill that space with more of himself. It's not necessarily a fun process to go through but the result is well worth it.

It was the following month before I was in any kind of shape to approach Teri and tell her what I had discovered about my anger. I told her I realized it was not a character flaw in me, it was bigger, MUCH bigger, and that it controlled me all these years.

I explained the steps I was taking to address the problem and then I looked at her and started to apologize. I was completely humbled knowing my anger was such a wicked driving force in our marriage and relationship. I knew the harm that it caused her.

In my remorse, I ended up laying on her lap for well over an hour, crying, as I apologized for my behavior telling her "I'm sorry. I'm so sorry, Teri" repeatedly. The instances I could remember when I was especially hurtful to her I apologized for specifically, but the overwhelming feeling that came over me was to say simply, "I'm sorry" and "I was wrong."

As I lay there, I felt completely humbled as a man knowing my actions and inability to control my anger hurt her so much.

Teri seemed somewhat indifferent to the whole episode. She stroked my hair gently as I lay in her lap but she did not really say much to me the entire time I was crying and apologizing. I imagine she had heard my apologies over my angry outburst before (though seldom) and perhaps she thought this was simply another one of those times.

As I said earlier, the last brick was laid in the wall *I built* around Teri's heart when she told me she wanted a divorce, and she was not going to let me in ever again and take a chance on me hurting her.

Fair enough.

I had made my bed over the past three decades and now was going to have to lie in it. I had no one to blame but myself and I didn't. My anger had gotten me to this point and it was my issue and mine alone to deal with. Whatever the future held for my marriage, it was completely out of my control.

"It's More Than an Anger Issue."

The following day began just as any other morning had the past few weeks. While still lying in bed, I would pray and then realize the situation I was in and an overwhelming sense of loss would overcome me.

This particular morning, I slid out of bed and knelt with my face to the floor while crying uncontrollably, as I asked the Lord once again to help me. These cries for help did not center on help for my marriage or for help for anything other than for *me*. I knew *me*, as a person, was in trouble, that I had no way out of my mess in my own strength. It was a cry of total surrender.

I don't know how long I laid there, minutes, perhaps ten, fifteen, maybe 30. Time wasn't a factor during these sessions of purging, just as when you're sick and draped over the toilet, you're not thinking about time. You just want whatever it is making you sick OUT of your body.

It was during these times that I felt completely alone, completely isolated from the world, and I can't really say with honesty that I even felt God was with me, but I knew from His promises in the Bible He was.

I didn't really have conscious thoughts during these purge sessions; again, just as if I draped myself over the toilet —all I could think about was getting whatever was inside me out, I couldn't identify what it was that I needed to get out. It was a sickness, no doubt about it, but it was a sickness of my soul and of my heart, that was leaving me. All I could do was lay there —just like a dam with a breach, and let it flow out of me until it determined it was time to stop.

What occurred next will forever be cemented in my mind for the rest of my life. As I laid there, completely powerless and completely at the will of whatever it was willing me, I heard a voice, not an audible voice, but a 'voice' all the same. It said calmly to me "Austin, you know that anger issue you have? It's more than an anger issue, you are emotionally abusive."

BAM! With the blinding flash and power of a lightning bolt hitting me, I instantly realized the whole truth of whom and what I was. I felt as if my legs had been hacked from beneath me and I was reduced to ZERO. I was NOTHING—I was less than nothing.

For the first time in my life, I could clearly see in my mind all the hundreds of times I was abusive to Teri. Not in individual scenes but rather a complete awareness of all that I had done to her, and the truth of the abusive man I was for as long as I could remember.

It's as if I was standing in a totally glassed-in room, trying to look through blinds that covered everything and POOF, in a flash, the blinds were gone and I could see, for the first time in my life, the crystal clear landscape of abuse that was all around me, previously hidden by darkness and disguise.

Despite the dazzling array of awareness projecting in my head, my mind was clear and more sharply focused than it had been in months... years. My immediate reaction was not one of shock or disbelief or going into hysterics. I simply lay there, crying, and for the first time in my life... *knowing*.

"Then you will know the truth, and the truth will set you free."

Everything I thought I knew about myself was reduced to rubble; destroyed in an instant. In my mind I was the lowest form of life known to man; I was someone who was a predator, someone who took advantage of innocent people and did as I pleased for my own gain.

The absolute shame I felt was immeasurable. I WAS A BAD PERSON. I had no worth to anyone - as a man, husband and father - I was nothing, I knew nothing, I had nothing. I laid there with close eyes and a thousand mile stare, slowly shaking my head back and forth, as I allowed the reality of the truth to wash over and through me, internalizing itself into every bone and fiber of my body.

I have no idea how long this lasted but eventually, I fell asleep or passed out, right on the floor of our bedroom.

Humbly Facing the Truth

The rest of the day was a blur to me but I knew what I had to do at the first opportunity —I had to tell Teri.

Later that evening, as she was getting ready for bed in the extra bedroom (we were not sleeping in the same room at this point), I asked if I could speak to her.

I could tell by my facial expression she sensed something was up and it was something out of the ordinary. She sat up, leaned back against the wall and drew her knees up so I could sit down. I sat on the bed at her feet, looked her in the eyes, drew a deep breath and humbly explained to her what was revealed to me earlier that morning; the truth – that my anger went way beyond 'anger'; I admitted I was emotionally abusive to her for as long as I could remember and that I will forever be sorry to her for what I did.

She sat patiently and as I unfolded the story of what transpired hours earlier, she leaned her head into her hands and began to cry... sob—her shoulders heaving up and down. I leaned my forehead on her knees and said with my own sobbing voice, "I am so sorry Teri. For all I've done to you over the years."

After a moment or two, we both looked at each other with tear stained eyes. I could see the relief on her face. She told me she had known for some time I was abusive.

About fifteen years prior, she signed up to volunteer at a house for battered women and as part of her training learned about the different forms of abuse, the traits of an abusive person, and the effects on the victim.

Upon hearing me admit to her, in my own words, that I was abusive, she was validated after all the years; she wasn't crazy; it wasn't her fault; she wasn't the one to blame as I unmercifully tried to convince her all those years.

It was a tender few moments for us both; confirmation for Teri and for the first time I could ever remember, I allowed myself to be completely vulnerable to my wife. Though it was a new experience for me, I liked how it felt.

I leaned forward, held my kiss on her forehead for a few moments, lifted her chin and looked her in the eyes and apologized once more, and then left the room to allow her time to process a marriage chock-full of misery... finally "outed" in all its ugly truth.

Chapter 5
First Steps to Recovery

Guilt upon the conscience, like rust upon iron, both defiles and consumes it, gnawing and creeping into it, as that does which at last eats out the very heart and substance of the metal. __South

The days following my admission of guilt were somber around our household. There was a sense of peace for the first time but certainly no joy, even though the 30-year bondage that strangled our marriage was broken, or at least revealed.

The divorce was still looming and I spent most days walking around in a fog—I didn't know what to do with myself. It was a time of deep reflection and personal regret knowing I allowed such a darkness to invade my mind and our home—that I wasn't able to recognize it for what it was until now.

I kept asking myself "Why" repeatedly. Why did this happen to me? Where and when did I take such an evil detour along the road of life? I mean, I was a good kid. Really was. I never gave my parents trouble, did what I was supposed to do and followed the rules. My childhood seemed normal; I felt I came from a loving home and my parents provided for my needs. Yes, my father died when I was young, but I thought I handled it as best I could and came through the loss okay.

Where did I fall apart? For a few years following my dad's death I experimented with alcohol and drugs during my time in the military, but the use stopped a short time after marrying Teri since she had nothing to do with drugs of any kind.

The alcohol never became more than a social consumption for either of us. Deep down inside I *always* knew right from wrong and felt I was a good person growing up. Where did it, and I, all unravel and when did I fall asleep and allow myself to fall into the dark and dank pit of domestic violence?

I had no idea how all this played out in Teri's head either. I knew she needed time to absorb and process what I told her and what it all meant - to her and to us - and I was not about to push her on the subject. I figured when she was ready to talk about it, she'd let me know.

My days were filled mostly with just trying to survive while trying to come to grips with the last three decades of my life - I was completely numb to all else.

It was if for the vast majority of my life I was stuck in a dream, a nightmare, and I suddenly woke up and found myself in a reality that was foreign to me yet all the people and situations of the nightmare came into my new reality - the only thing different was 'me'.

I somehow felt detached from the person who was abusive for all those years, for that person was not the *real me*, yet the *real me* was faced with all the damage and destruction that person created.

To say I was remorseful would be an understatement. It's impossible to convey in words what I felt those first days and weeks, knowing the damage I alone caused in the lives of the three people I love the most on this planet. The very ones, who trusted me to love, cherish and provide for them. It was if my whole life was a sham.

Nearly all of the major abuse symptoms I exhibited for so long were broken off me that Monday morning on the floor. Anger, criticism, manipulation, the need to control, looking at myself as a rescuer, as well as my Jekyll-Hyde personality, all relinquished their control over me.

That's not to say I didn't have battles over the coming months with some of those old nemeses whom I nurtured for so long, but their power to control and jerk my strings as a puppeteer while I remained helpless were gone.

I knew I needed professional help in the worst way to handle all that I woke up to, but I didn't have a clue who or where to turn to get it. Most days I spent on my knees praying and crying. I had so much evil and evil deeds built up in my heart over three decades.

It was as if the slimy, filthy goop that coated the very lining of my soul needed scraped off and purged before anything good could be put back in me.

The only method I had to purge that evil was via tears. I cried buckets... barrels. The tears were all tears of remorse and humility – from a man, forty-eight-years-old, who realized what a waste his life had been to that point. They were tears of a deep, desperate plea for help. From the only one who *could* help me – my Lord.

It was terrible not being able to share my thoughts, feelings, and experiences with Teri. The one whom I so much wanted to go to and hug and give words of comfort to - not that I knew what 'comfort' words to say exactly - but perhaps just a simple "We'll get through this."

I wanted to share how the "old me" was gone and a "new me" was present, but it wasn't an option extended to me. Teri's heart remained sealed off to me and with it, any sense of compassion or willingness to listen. I knew I couldn't push or force her feelings. I had to sit back, wait, and hope that somehow, someway, the wall around her heart would begin to weaken, just a crack, and eventually, with LOTS of love, time and commitment, crumble.

During the coming weeks, however, I began to realize it was not to be. Teri remained distant from me emotionally. It was as if she was operating on some sort of autopilot as she went through each day, her emotions stuck in a persistent flat-line, never allowing herself to entangle in the actuality of the truth revealed.

She soon shared with me that my recent admission of emotional abuse was evidence of a "green light" from God to continue the pursuit of a divorce - not exactly, the words I was hoping to hear for sure. I asked her if it was possible God revealed all this to us, at this exact point in time, so that we would stay together and work to build a healthy marriage. "No" was her response.

Crushed, I felt within my spirit that what she spoke was not the truth, but I had no choice but to accept that what she said were her honest feelings and continue on the path that I had to travel in order to get healthy.

A Plea for Help Answered

One day, I was flipping through channels on the television (rarely do I watch TV) when a woman on a talk show caught my eye. I decided to tune-in for a few moments to check out what she was talking about, but I soon lost interest in the subject matter so I went about my day.

In a strange twist of fate, I found myself later in the day surfing her website, trying to find out what other topics she discussed. I came across a couple video interviews she did with a person who battered his wife.

Normally I would skip right over something like that because, though abusive, I definitely wasn't a batterer and frankly in my current mental state, I didn't want to listen to some guy talk about how he messed up some other woman's life—been there done that. However, I pushed the play button and half listened as I went about doing other work on the computer.

Most of his talk about extreme physical violence towards his wife did not catch my attention, but when he started to discuss certain aspects of an abusive person's behavior my ears perked up. I saw myself and my situation in what he talked about. I was amazed at what I heard from this person, Dr. Paul Hegstrom.

Could some cross wiring in my brain somehow explain all that happened within me? Could whatever was *done* be *undone*? What was "Arrested Development" he mentioned? I called Dr. Hegstrom's office and after a few minutes discussion about the program he offered, called Life Skills (more on that later), was fortunate enough to find one offered in my hometown.

I called the facilitator of the program in my town, Jim, to find out more information. Jim was a very laid-back, unflappable sort of man who spoke with a slow cadence and slight southern drawl in his kind voice. He began the conversation by asking me to explain my situation. As I mentally prepared to answer, I realized I had no idea how to summarize my experience of the last 30 years in just a few sentences.

After several awkward, fumbling minutes on my part, I seemed to give some semblance of an answer and we continued a discussion along with several more back and forth questions. It seemed I was a good candidate for the six month program, however, Jim explained to me that a class had already started four weeks prior and they had a strict policy not to allow anyone to join a class in progress.

As I hung up the phone I felt deflated and dejected, but there wasn't much I could do about it. After all, rules were rules and Jim was not particularly inclined to break them just for me.

A few minutes later, as I sat and tried to figure out what and where to go next, I remembered I didn't find out about the costs of the program, so I decided to call Jim back and ask. After he told me the financial particulars, he paused a few moments and said, "You really want in this program don't you?" I broke down crying as I choked out "I just want to stop hurting."

Jim, in his wisdom and compassion, agreed to speak to the men in the current class about my joining them even though against policy. He explained to me that group cohesiveness and trust was vital to the healing; that by bringing someone in after four weeks it might jeopardize that cohesiveness as well as any bonding that had taken place.

Jim told me he could not make any promises, it was up to the other men in the class, but he would check and let me know. After a few tense days wait, Jim called back and informed me the class agreed that I could join them the following week.

Almost two months after my sickness revealed itself to me, I finally had hope of getting the help I so desperately needed. I will forever be indebted to Jim for what he did for me during the darkest time of my life. He and I remain friends to this day.

A New Beginning

My class time in Life Skills was a much-needed tonic for my soul. I learned a great deal about abusive behavior, victims of abuse, relationships, family dynamics, and I learned how the mind plays such a relevant role in all of it. I quickly bonded with my dozen or so classmates and enjoyed Jim's teachings.

I felt like I was in a safe environment amongst like-minded people I could trust. Everyone in the class, students as well as facilitators, were either abusers or previous abusers. We all could relate to each other's stories, mindsets, and for some, excuses. I ate it all up as if a kid in a candy store. I craved to know what happened to me and more importantly, I needed to know how to recover from it. I needed to know how to repair the damage I caused Teri and the girls.

In the class I could talk freely about my issues and many times I held classmates accountable for their own abusive behavior, which meant I was learning. Accountability was something we all did for each other but for some, it was very easy to slip into a victim mentality and start blaming their wife or others for their own bad behaviors.

In many ways, I felt blessed in the manner my abuse revealed itself to me, because from that moment forward, I never once thought about Teri's issues at all. I was broken and knew that I was responsible for the demise of my marriage and it left me a very humble man.

After several weeks of classes, I began to get a confidence that inside I truly was a different person. I still had trouble dealing with the inner-child that remained locked within, but how I handled the moments of insecurity and fear was completely different – I didn't fly off the handle and into an angry rage.

I suppose to some extent the numbness I consistently felt in my mind helped, but I could tell my entire focus changed as well as my thought processes. I no longer concentrated on everyone else's problems, - I focused on *my* problems and *me*.

It was apparent however, that Teri was not prepared to drop any of the defensive walls she had built up around herself the last few months. We drudged through the daily routines of home life okay, but it seemed everyone had withdrawn into their own survival mode. I was still dazed and confused, trying to get a handle on my nightmare and had regular periods of purging uncontrollably.

Despite my new confidence of being a new person, an overwhelming sense of gloom hung over me as I faced the state of my marriage and the knowledge I did not have a chance to share with Teri what I was going through. I desperately wanted her to know, so that somehow she could believe that what I told her had happened to me was in fact true. Rather, she seemed to be almost void of *any* feelings toward me at this point.

The girls and Teri seemed to huddle together more than normal and even the times we sat down at the family dinner table were strained and somewhat awkward. The "How did your day go?" question was not asked as it normally was. No longer were we a family, even at its dysfunctional best. We appeared to be four individuals sharing the same house, or probably more accurately, three people and one boarder – with me being the boarder.

This was very understandable and justified given the distance between Teri and I. I was withdrawn as I desperately tried to figure out a way to fit back into the family dynamics, while at the same time dealing with all the emotions constantly banging around inside my head. My constant state of anger was gone but I still felt like a pressure cooker without a relief valve.

I felt bad for my two girls. Not only was their family security blown apart by the impending divorce, but their father was a shell of the man he once was –completely broken. Many days they saw me with a deer in the headlights look on my face or they heard me purging in another room. Their world was rocked on many different levels and all at the same time.

I don't pretend to know what all they experienced during those months, but I'm sure some of the wounds in their heart and soul remain, even five years later.

I knew in my heart after a few short weeks that the proper thing to do was to move out and give Teri and the kids the space and time they needed to try and get things back to some semblance of "normal" - whatever that was at this point. There were simply too many things to deal with, all going on at the same time, and I did not see things getting better with the current family dynamics.

Around the first part of July I approached Teri and told her what was on my mind as far as moving out —she didn't disagree. Within a couple of weeks, I found a friend who said I could move into the spare bedroom of a house he converted into an office building for his insurance business.

I thought it best to move out on a weekday so that the kids would be gone from the house and Teri would be at work. I could take my time figuring out the minimal things I needed to take with me without them being around—it seemed like the least dramatic way to leave.

My last day in the house, I sat on the front porch cooling down after my morning walk when Teri came out to join me. We kept the conversation upbeat and positive and that seemed to suit both of us just fine. After all, how do you say goodbye to someone you shared a life with for the past 30 years? "See you later" doesn't seem to cut it at a time like this.

After several minutes of conversation Teri simply stood, tears welling up in her eyes, walked over, tenderly kissed me on the forehead, said "goodbye"... and went into the house.

And so it was, with mixed emotions and a heavy heart, that I moved away that day from the people I love the most and the 4-bedroom house in the suburbs that we shared as a family for the previous twelve years. Twenty-four years of being a united family was coming to an end... and it hurt.

My new 'home' was a 10' x 10' bedroom located on the lower level of my friend's tri-level house/office. I had use of the kitchen on the main level of the office before and after business hours, but would have to find a way to make do without an oven (since it was against code to have one in a business for some reason).

Overall, the price was right and it gave me a chance to be alone and attempt to get my head screwed back on while I attended my Life Skills classes. It also gave Teri and the girls the breathing room I knew they needed.

It was a new beginning to my life perhaps, but not one I was looking forward to.

Chapter 6
The Old Austin
Makes an Appearance

The guilt that feels not its own shame is wholly incurable. –It was the redeeming promise in the fault of Adam that with the commission of his crime came the sense of his nakedness. __Simms

I continued my weekly classes and tried to love Teri, without any strings attached, as best I could. Once I moved out, I tried to do things for her and at times, asked if I could come over and do things around the house in order to give her a hand since she was working full time.

A few times, I did her laundry while I was over at the house doing mine while she was at work. Overall, it was awkward, but I was determined to serve and love her as best I could - no matter how she felt or acted towards me.

I know it is easy to think that I was trying to win her back or in some sick way trying to manipulate her, but that was not the case. Never in my life had I witnessed Teri so shut down, so emotionally void of all life it seemed, anytime I was around her.

She was cordial when we were together, but remained distant and on-guard the whole time. I was getting exactly what I deserved of course, but I still could not help wanting to love her and do for her until inevitably, what I knew in my heart was to come, the end of our relationship.

No, there was no agenda in what I did for her those few months, other than a broken husband trying to love his wife as he should have, and wished he could have, from day one.

Out with the New, In with the Old

Though I was hurting tremendously due to the impending divorce, the breakup of our family, and the continual realization of the pain I caused everyone, I also had brief moments of true joy. I knew without a doubt the changes that occurred within me the past several months were genuine; they were not forced, planned, or rehearsed – it was the new 'who' that I was now - and it felt fantastic! I felt free!

I still had a long way to go to conquer some of the old, abusive tendencies that flashed in my mind occasionally, but the overwhelming 'hum' in my mind was a freedom to love - in a way I never was able to love before. I loved my wife and children not for what I would get out of it, but just because it felt good to do so.

I knew I would be okay, I was not going to climb back into the skin of the monster I was before. Yes, there would be many hiccups and stumbles along the way, but I knew the power emotional abuse had over me for 30-years was broken!

I was no longer powerless to the control and no longer unaware of my behavior, no longer unaware when I said or did something that possibly hurt others —it was a great feeling, I was very thankful to be set free.

Yet, despite it all, I still didn't know the 'how' and the 'why' of how it all occurred. That revelation was still a few weeks away. But first, there was to be an encounter with an old, dark acquaintance who made an encore appearance, just to say "Hi" and see how I would respond.

One evening during our high school senior night football game, (our youngest daughter was a cheerleader), the old Austin made a sudden, and dramatic appearance. Senior night is when all the senior football players, cheerleaders, and support personnel are escorted onto the field by their family and introduced to the crowd.

As our family lined up to go onto the field, Teri made a comment to me - nothing bad, just a 'wifely' comment - but instantly, a button got pushed within me. Wires, still connected to an area of behavior I thought was permanently disconnected, somehow short-circuited and completed an old circuit in my mind - I got mad and went silent on everyone. My inner-child didn't know how to handle the situation.

I knew my family noticed what happened, they had seen this a hundred times in the past. Through unspoken words, I sensed an underlying fear or perhaps in my mind, a condescending "I knew it!" emanating from each one of them as if they knew, eventually, I would fail and fall back to my old ways. I was once again that powerless puppet, moving and thinking at the whims of that evil puppeteer who controlled me.

It was a very awkward moment as we walked across the field and the timing was absolutely the worst! I hated that I felt I ruined my daughter's Senior Night but I could not break the hold the puppeteer had on me.

After the game, I spent very little time visiting, all I wanted to do at that moment was get away from the situation and my family as fast as I could before something else went wrong. I had no idea how what just happened occurred, but there was nothing to gain by me sticking around.

During the drive to my place, I went back to my 'cave' mentality and every past transgression Teri had 'done to me' poured through my mind like a View Master snapping off frames at warp-speed. I got home and collapsed in my chair, totally bewildered and dejected at the same time yet trying to battle the overwhelming thoughts spinning through my mind.

I was losing the fight big time. Somehow, I was blindsided by an old pattern and now it was in control again... I was scared, and I was pissed!

After a while of not making any progress, I decided to go to bed and hope for a better day tomorrow, or maybe there would be no tomorrow - that would be okay too.

I numbly climbed into bed, turned out the lights and as soon as my head hit the pillow, that inner voice in my heart said, "You go apologize to her." As weird as this will sound to some (and completely understandable to others), at the exact moment those words were spoken to me, I was moving out of bed to find my jacket and keys; both the words and the movement happened in a single, fluid motion.

In a few moments, I realized that I was once again a puppet at the hands of a puppeteer, but I knew this time God was in charge.

I could tell Teri seemed ticked at me when I called to ask if I could stop by for "Sixty seconds." She finally agreed even though it was late and I had ruined the evening.

When I got to the house, I sat across from Teri on the front porch, looked into those beautiful, brown eyes and humbly said, "I'm sorry Teri. My behavior was wrong tonight. I apologize and ask for your forgiveness." She thought for a few moments before she accepted the apology, and that was the end of our conversation.

As I got up to leave, I said, "I don't know what happened, but the old Austin made an appearance tonight. I guess I have a long way to go in my recovery from all this." I kissed her on the forehead and left.

This was a huge breakthrough for me! Yes, I slide back into the old Austin skin and yes, I was completely powerless to its control, but somehow, knowing there was nothing to do but humbly apologize and the way I apologized, broke something further within me – in a good way.

When I apologized to Teri, I gave no justification for my behavior – I said I was sorry; I was wrong and asked for her forgiveness. I didn't try to give a reason for my actions as I did so many times in the past.

Normally, my apology would be something like this, "Sorry I got so upset at the game last night. I had a bad day at work and the way you said what you did set me off." Do you see the difference? With this kind of apology, not only did I wait until the next day to apologize, giving time for hurt feelings to turn to bitterness, but I did not accept any responsibility for the way I behaved.

It was the "bad day at work," along with the way Teri said her comment to me that caused me to act the way I acted.

No matter how another person acts towards us, or the kind of day we are having, if we act wrongly we must apologize for our wrongs, not give a thinly veiled "Sorry," followed by all the 'valid reasons' we acted the way we did.

I hated the way I acted at the game earlier and though it wasn't me who initiated the idea of the apology, it was me who allowed myself to be completely humbled and sincerely sorry for my behavior as I sat before my wife. No hidden agenda, no hoping to hear the "That's all right" acceptance phrase from her.

My self-worth wasn't dependent on whether she forgave me or not. I screwed up big-time but I handled it in the best, most humble way I could, and that's all I can expect out of myself. My inner-child didn't force me to run and hide; I faced this as an adult!

I do not mean to imply this was the first time since my recovery that I faced something as an adult, but it was the first time my old behavior made such a drastic appearance in front of my entire family, yet I ended up handling it as an adult.

In the past, due to shame, guilt, insecurity, and fear of rejection, I would have run and hidden in my cave for days because I didn't know how to deal with my feelings.

I probably would have hidden behind my mask of anger, trying in some way to place the guilt and the blame on Teri so she would apologize for what she said to me. Teri had no problem dealing with her emotions. This would take the place of me having to deal with mine, or more accurately, my inability to deal with mine.

Tonight, circumstances forced me to face all those feelings and emotions, process them, and apologize for them. It was a huge relief allowing myself to be this vulnerable to Teri. Vulnerable because I was giving her full control whether she chose to accept the apology or reject it, rejecting me along the way.

As I drove back home, as bad as I had acted at the game, I felt good about how the evening ended up, and I felt good about myself.

"Too little too Late"

A couple bright spots happened as winter and the holidays approached - I got full-time, temporary work and I was able to move into a house prior to Christmas, thanks to another friend of mine. Getting a job got my butt up and moving in a regular, daily routine rather than sulking.

Getting out of that 10' x 10' hole and into a more normal pattern of living helped me feel better about my situation. I bought a Christmas tree, decorated it and had the kids over a couple times too. It was good therapy for me.

It was also during this time, in one of my final classes, that all the pieces to my abusive puzzle fit together. I finally got all the answers as to "how" and "why" my abusive behavior started. It was a wonderful revelation - one that took me completely by surprise. I will detail it and other roots to my abusive behavior in the next chapter.

With those final pieces, I had everything I needed to heal completely from my past torment.

Shortly thereafter, Teri told me separation was no longer an option for her and she wanted to go ahead and divorce. Her decision did not necessarily surprise me but at the same time, it disappointed me.

I sincerely hoped and prayed that with the changes she saw in me over the previous four months, real, life-changing changes, that had to be emanating from inside me instead of some 'plastic' facade I was wearing in an attempt to fool her. I hoped she might hold off longer and see how things progressed. But it was not to be, her mind was made up.

It was not long after hearing her words, as the underlying reality of my divorce drew nearer, that the tentacles of depression tightened their grip around me, and pulled me back into the abyss of its darkness. I could not shake the feeling I had in my soul that despite the problems Teri and I had all the years of our marriage, divorce was not the right answer in this situation.

It just didn't make sense that God would break me free from the hell of my abuse after all these years and transform me, all while Teri and I were still together, just to have it be the final act in our marriage.

I kept thinking what a great testimony this could be - two people, due to emotional abuse, taken to the brink of divorce yet through the healing power of the Lord, found a way to allow Him to rebuild and heal areas in their lives each did not have the strength to rebuild or heal on their own.

As kind of a confirmation, a few weeks later as my best friend and I were moving some things out of the house, he said through tears "This isn't right. This just isn't right."

With our divorce date looming, I made one last, desperate, written plea to Teri, asking her not to go through with it. I asked her to allow more time for us to mend our differences, and asked her to consider that the intent of the separation was to give our situation more time before deciding termination of the marriage and our family was the only, and best solution.

Despite my current and dark state of mind, I saw a bright future for Teri and I once we weathered this storm and felt very confident we could recoup all that was lost and have a very strong marriage going forward. I still loved Teri dearly and for the first time in my life knew *how* to love her.

However, I think Teri was facing some of her own deeply rooted issues stemming from the relationship with her abusive mother and by NOT divorcing me, perhaps she thought she would never break free of the bondage her mother still held over her.

Perhaps she felt by going through with our divorce she was exhibiting strength that would allow her to recover, in some way, all that my abuse and the abuse suffered during her childhood stole from her.

I knew Teri saw a radical transformation in me over the previous seven months yet I could not fault her for her feelings. I knew divorce was not the right answer, but after all I had done to her over three decades, how could I fault her for anything she felt she needed to do?

Teri told me soon after my plea, "I've seen changes in you, but I don't trust them. It's too little too late. I have to do this."

And so it was, after all she and I had been through, a few weeks later, Mr. and Mrs. James Austin were no more.

Chapter 7
The Root Cause of my Abusive Behavior

Behavior is a mirror in which everyone displays his image. __Goethe

What caused these abusive traits in me? Was I born this way, did some gene defect in my family lineage pass down over the years from one generation to the next? Was it a childhood trauma? Did I simply wake up one day and think control and manipulation were the secret to happiness?

Why do I see so many men with some of the same abusive behaviors I exhibited walking around thinking they are a "great, stand-up guy" like I used to think?

My early childhood was what I would call normal. My dad had a very good career so we were not lacking for anything. Two kids, two cars, beautiful house in suburbia, family vacation every year, life was good. Dad worked a lot while mom stayed home to take care of the house and us kids.

My sister was four years older than I was so she and I never became close. She was the rebel of the family and I was the happy, carefree kid who never really caused my parents any problems. I did what I was told, when I was told to, and did it to the best of my ability.

My mom and I had fun being around each other; she always took care of me and made me the best cheese sandwiches for lunch that any kid could have.

Due to my dad's line of work, my mom and dad had many friends and there always seemed to be something going on at our house. It was a fun childhood as I remember, a decent representation of the 'American Dream' I suppose.

One day, during my early teen years, that all came to a screeching halt when my dad was diagnosed with Leukemia. Back then, there wasn't Google or the Internet, so I didn't really know what Leukemia was, but I didn't remember my dad being sick a day in his life so I didn't give this particular sickness a lot of concern nor did I think he wouldn't get well.

My mother was out of town at the hospital most of the time so I guess her not being around much helped to not alert me that something was up.

One time, my uncle came into to town to see my family while we all visited my dad. This was the first time I had a chance to visit him since he had gotten sick and admitted to the hospital.

During my uncle's visit, he told me that my dad needed some kind of bone marrow transplant and things were serious, that there was a possibility my dad might not make it. I don't know if it was the way my uncle said it or whether I just was not able to believe it, but those words - "might not make it" - didn't fully register with me at the time.

I was a pretty naïve kid and there wasn't anything my dad couldn't do, so I went back home after my visit and continued with my daily school life and being the happy, carefree kid I was... right up till the time I went to visit my dad for the second time a few weeks later.

While waiting at the hospital to see him, I went downstairs to buy a Coke. As I got back off the elevator in the waiting area, a close family friend met me and said, "Austin... your dad, it's all over, he's gone."

Suddenly my happy, carefree life wasn't so happy nor was it so carefree.

I remember looking out the window of a small grieving room we were sent to in the hospital, looking down on all the people scurrying about outside, thinking, *How can all you people be going about your day as if nothing happened? Don't you know my dad just died?*

My dad's death affected my life in a deep, dark, mysterious way for the next three decades.

Three specific things happened to and within me that reshaped me into someone completely different than the happy, carefree kid I once knew. Three things crippled my mind and in turn, crippled me.

I wasn't crippled in a physical sense, with visible evidence showing my inabilities.   No, that type of crippling would have brought immediate treatment.

I was crippled in the invisible realm of my mind, where it is much more difficult to diagnose and treat abnormalities. My crippling wasn't immediate following my trauma either... like a slow spreading cancer, it took a few years to cripple that naïve, happy, carefree mind into the abusive horror that hide within me for so many years.

Arrested Development

I discuss Arrested Development in more detail later, but I wanted to give a *brief* overview of it now because it was one of three major contributors that led to my life of emotional abuse.

I was an emotionally immature kid and had not completed puberty by the time of my dad's death. Most of the physical attributes were present but I had not developed the psychological tools I needed to function as an adult.

There is no need for us to have the ability to process things as it relates to the 'big picture' of life, for instance, how to handle conflict with others, when our entire life consists of eating, sleeping, and pooping. Yep, things are simple during our early years.

As we grow physically, we slowly develop our mental processes and are given the emotional tools we need at the age we need them, give or take a few years.

The plan is by the time we reach adulthood; we possess a fully developed physical and mental framework, which allows us to tackle life's challenges on our own.

If a traumatic event (molestation, physical abuse, rejection, death, etc.) happens in a child's life at an early age, when the child has not yet developed some of the psychological tools they will need during adulthood, the trauma of that event can freeze their emotional development at whatever stage it was in when the trauma occurred.

The child will of course continue to mature physically, but emotionally they will process their world at whatever age they were at when the emotional development locked. They may be an adult on the outside, but they cannot reason nor process things as an adult.

If you think of the mind as a big computer, it's like during computer start up when sometimes the computer will hang or freeze and not continue beyond a certain point of the boot up sequence (if you're a PC user, you know exactly what I'm talking about - Mac users, not so much).

No matter what you try to do, short of turning the power to the computer off, the computer locks and is not going to progress any further until you figure out what went wrong.

For the victim of Arrested Development, their emotional computer froze during the developmental boot up and it is not going to go past whatever stage of the startup process it was in until someone figures out what went wrong and fixes it.

Although I was fifteen-years-old when my dad died, emotionally I had not developed past the age of twelve-years or so. Due to the trauma of my dad's death, my emotional development froze at that age – twelve.

As I grew through my teens and into adulthood and eventually marriage, I looked and talked as the adult I was, but I managed my world through the eyes and mind of a twelve-year-old child. A twelve-year-old mind isn't quite equipped to handle such feelings and emotions as insecurity, rejection, fear, inadequacy, conflict, frustration, or anger, just to name a few.

Yes, they have been exposed to most of these feelings and emotions and are *beginning* to learn to handle them but, they certainly have not reached the level of emotional maturity needed to process them as a self-sufficient adult, they still need supervision and guidance.

My Arrested Development manifested itself not long after my dad died. Here is a good example: I always had a good technological aptitude and knew I wanted to be involved with computers and technology when I grew up. Upon graduating high school, I enrolled in a local college that offered an excellent computer sciences program.

I was still living at home at the time so I was eligible to receive monthly checks from my dad's Social Security. I had a car, a great girl I was interested in, some money in the bank each month, and a promising education and career ahead of me. Now I realize eighteen-year-old kids are not the most emotionally developed creatures walking the face of this planet, but if I would have stopped and evaluated my life for a moment, things were not that bad, all things considered.

After just two quarters at college however, a friend and I one day, unexpectedly and with zero forethought, decided we would both go down to the Army recruitment center and enlist. If that was not bad enough, I had no idea what I wanted to do while I was in the Army! I walked in and said "I want to do the toughest job you offer." I did not look at brochures, no talking with the recruiter about my life plans and goals, nothing.

One day I was a civilian with no aspirations of military life and the next, a Private First Class getting ready to head to boot camp. Fortunately, after I got out I was still able to salvage a good career in the technical field, but it was a lot of work. And I certainly don't regret serving my country those four years, I think everyone should serve at least two, but on that day my friend and I decided to enlist, I didn't stop for two seconds and think about what I was doing or what I was giving up, or what I was getting in to for that matter. All I could think about was the 'here and now,' how much fun it would be to enlist. Sounds like something a twelve-year-old would do.

My Arrested Development kept me locked emotionally as a child for 33 years. I was completely deceived the entire time, thinking I was handling my life pretty well considering my circumstances. Except the truth was, I didn't know how to effectively handle *any* area of my life.

As Teri and I progressed from dating to marriage, I never fully developed the ability to deal with my own feelings and emotions, much less how to deal with hers at the same time as her husband.

I was not good at conflict resolution because I looked at everything as a child, which meant I focused on ME. I didn't know how to step back and look at things from both viewpoints and try to figure out a win-win solution; I always put the priority on *my* viewpoint and could only dimly see Teri's viewpoint.

When something came up or Teri said something that I could not deal with, I simply shutdown and withdrew, or I blew up in a manic rage. I would then withdraw to my cave and stew about *her*, rather than thinking about *my* transgressions. Everything in my life - marriage, career, finances, relationships, etc., were all touched negatively due to my emotional retardation and inability to manage issues as an adult.

Life Commandment

Most of the memories of the days, weeks, and months immediately following my dad's death are sealed and stored in a hidden compartment within my mind, as my automated protection systems function as they were designed.

However, I can remember an incident that happened soon after he died very clearly. I was in my bedroom when our neighbor next door, Jan, stopped by to talk to me. Her middle son and I became hard and fast friends after my family moved in next door to them a few years ago.

I can still see Jan leaning against the door frame of my bedroom, talking to me as I fiddled with clothes in my closet. The conversation is a long forgotten memory, except for one innocent sentence she said that stuck in my mind - she said, "You know, you're the man of the family now." Just one simple sentence, one that people say all the time in these situations because they don't really know what to say, yet for me, that single, simple sentence became a *life commandment*.

A life commandment can be any phrase said, even a single time, that "sticks" or creates an "indelible stamp" in the mind of a child. Some sample phrases are:

- "Who do you think you are?"

- "Are you stupid?"

- "You'll never amount to anything."

- "Shut up!"

- "Quit bothering me."

- "You're just like your mother/father."

- "Act your age!"

- "You just like attention."

- "You're not as sharp as your sister in _____. " (Name the subject)

- "You always have trouble with _____." (Fill in the blank)

- "No one will ever love you as much as I do."

- "I wish you were never born."

Any one of hundreds of phrases like these that if said to a child A SINGLE TIME can imprint on their mind as a commandment. Something they will subconsciously follow the rest of their lives. A blueprint if you will.

There are no absolute rules that explain why a statement can be said to a child dozens and dozens of times yet not take root in their mind while other times, the same statement, said exactly at the right moment in time, becomes a life commandment to that child.

Most people realize, as parents, they need to be careful about what things get repeatedly said to their child. As the saying goes - when you hear something enough you begin to believe it.

I knew a couple who had a very attractive and vivacious daughter who never met a stranger and always had boys clamoring over her. She had a great upbringing with no obvious signs of trauma, yet for some reason, this young woman was never able to find the 'right guy'.

As it turns out, as a child, her father told her dozens of times "No one will love you as much as I do." Of course in the father's defense, he was only trying to reassure his daughter that she was loved and would always be taken care of, but he implanted in her mind a belief that no other man's love would ever measure up to his.

Normally, a life commandment is something said just once or only a few times. Perhaps in my situation I was living with such grief and pain that I was looking for someone, anyone, to give me words that would help sooth me. Perhaps my mind at the time my neighbor was speaking to me was very open to things she said because I really liked and respected her.

I don't know the specific 'how' or 'whys' but from that moment onward, that statement became my 'commandment' for life. It was as if a blueprint self-imposed in my mind and no matter what else happened during my lifetime, I was 'the man of the family' and my job was to take care of my mom.

Truth was, I *was not* the man of the family at all. I was a fifteen-year-old kid who suddenly and tragically lost my dad, the rock of my life, and I was scared to death. I was a boy who needed to run to my mommy and fall apart in her arms and be told that I would be nurtured and loved and be told everything would be alright; not someone whose job it was to 'be the man' and take care of my mom and sister, but that's what I thought I had to do.

My mother was still young when my dad died - mid-40's - and had plenty of time to pick herself up and put her life back together if she wanted to. She never wanted to. She never got over his death and she never got her focus off herself and her pain in order to give any reassurances to my sister and I that she could and would continue to take care of us and provide for us. As a result, I *did* think my job was to take of her, and 'be the man'.

Not long after my dad's death, my family moved back to our old hometown. It was a few years later when I decided to join the Army. I can remember as soon as I got to basic training I had to send money to my mom for her to live off of each month (my Social Security payments that I shared with my mom when I lived at home stopped when I dropped out of college).

The funny thing was though, my mom had decorators come in to decorate the new place and (I would find out later), she paid cash for the condominium we moved into.

The truth was my mom was accustomed to a lifestyle that my dad was able to provide and she never learned to ratchet that lifestyle down to fit her new monthly income. None of that registered in my mind however, so every month for the next four years I sent my mother a check.

To this day, I cringe when I hear a phrase that has the potential to become a life commandment spoken to a child. We never know when one of them might 'stick'.

When Son Becomes a Surrogate Husband

The life commandment and my Arrested Development were two big pieces of the puzzle that revealed to me how and why I became abusive. The third, last, and largest piece of the puzzle came to me completely unexpectedly one evening during a Life Skills class. It was to be the coup de grâce of my abusive life.

The title of the class was "The Mother/Son Relationship." *Great* I thought—*this should be interesting.*

After my dad died, my mother and I never seemed to be able to get back to the same great relationship we had before he died. It was almost as if she was not able to move forward with her life and she resented me because I was trying to move on with mine.

We would have some bad arguments from time to time and Teri would comment to me afterward that they must make me feel terrible due to some of the things my mom said to me. I used to shrug it off and simply say it only made me more hard-hearted towards my mom. Those 'hard-hearted' beliefs would change during the next hour and a half.

The main part of the class that evening was a video tape by Dr. Paul Hegstrom (founder of Life Skills) describing how the relationship between mother and son should develop as the son matures from childhood through puberty and into adulthood. He also explained how the family dynamics could shift should things go wrong during the son's maturation.

I should note this video was presented to me several years ago during a time of great emotional and psychological duress in my life. I probably do not remember all of the particulars of Dr. Hegstrom's presentation, but rather the areas that dealt with my particular situation. However, I hope to do justice to the Dr.'s presentation as I recall what I learned from it.

Please check the *Resource Section* for additional information on this bizarre and unknown form of abuse that I believe, in different forms and severities, is more common than we think. I have met several men whom I suspect, when they were a child, had some type of mother/son enmeshment issues with their mother.

There is a natural order to the family dynamics in a healthy family. When son and daughter are adolescents, son looks to father as his 'hero'; as the one he wants to pattern his life after. There is no one greater; the "My dad can beat up your dad" child's mentality.

Father is the one whom son looks to for approval and guidance at this stage of his life. Likewise, the daughter does the same with mother.

As puberty approaches, things shift. Son starts to discover 'girls' and awakens to the fact that his mother is one. Not in an unhealthy or unnatural way, but as changes naturally take place in his own body and brain, he begins to equate that mother is not only 'mom' but she's a 'girl' too. On a subconscious level, he begins to put a much higher value on getting love and acceptance from his mother.

Whereas before, son looked to father almost exclusively for guidance and acceptance, now he begins to look at mother. Father is not held in the highest esteem anymore.

As son becomes a bit older, mother is whom he patterns desirable qualities after when searching for a girlfriend and eventually a wife of his own (likewise for the father-daughter side of the equation). Daughter, while as an adolescent, patterns herself after mother but as puberty arrives, begins to shift her focus to father and his patterns as to what she looks for in a mate.

That is why the vast majority of time we see men marry women who are like their mother's, while women marry men who are like their father's. The qualities they look for in the opposite sex are patterned after their parents, whether those patterns are good or are bad.

During these years of puberty, son is especially vulnerable in his emotional development as his natural desire to seek out a nurturing, emotional, and sexual bond with the opposite sex begins to form within him. These feelings are all a bit foreign to this young man who not long ago thought *Girls have cooties!*

Of course within the family is mother, who is hopefully already in her own healthy and emotionally connected relationship with her husband. However, if a tragic event were to occur, perhaps through a death, or divorce or some other event that causes mother to have a sudden emotional detachment from her husband, a huge emotional vacuum forms within the mother. Her natural instinct is to seek out another emotional connection quickly to fill this void.

Precisely at a time when the emotionally vulnerable son is seeking a connection with a woman, mom, in her traumatized attempt to survive, may send "emotional requests" to her son in an attempt to fill her emotional vacuum. If son responds to these requests, subconsciously the glue is set and an emotional bridge is formed between them.

Mom now begins to feed off son for her emotional needs and soon discovers she has power and control over him. The son, not having developed the psychological capacity to know what is happening, has this underlying desire to "help mom out" and meet her emotional needs during her husband's absence.

A strong bond is formed between mother and son that gets stronger over time as mom's needs get stronger and stronger. Son is now filling in as her 'husband' on an emotional basis for his mother. He is her surrogate husband. In *extreme* cases (thank God mine was not one of them) this sick, mother-son bond can also lead to incest.

Our Creator gave man the capacity to fill the emotionally needs of one woman only. You may know someone who always seems to have multiple girlfriends at the same time but if he is being honest, there is only one of them that truly captures his heart - she is his single emotional bond.

There's also a Bible verse that speaks to this connection: "For this reason man will leave his father and mother and be united to his wife, and they will become one flesh." (Gen 2:24). Again, man is shown to have an emotional bond with only one woman.

While the son is locked in to provide for his mother's emotional needs, he has zero chance to form a normal emotional bond with any other woman, regardless of how close the physical bond may be, as long as this strong mother/son emotional connection exists.

As this unnatural connection continues, the son subconsciously hates these emotional bonds because they do not feel right to him and he is being controlled. He says to himself *No woman will ever do what this woman is doing to me.*

As his natural instincts prevail, and he gets involved with another woman, he will exert his control on her first in an attempt to prevent her from doing what his mother is doing to him. At this point, without being cognizant, the son starts to distrust and dislike other women (the term is "Misogynist").

You see, the son isn't able to comprehend in his subconscious that the unnatural emotional bond with his mother isn't the same one he would have with another woman outside his family, his subconscious only equates "female emotional bond = BAD."

As the relationship with this other woman develops, he starts to exert further control on her in order to weaken her so she won't be able to gain the upper hand in the relationship and do (he mistakenly thinks) what his mother is doing to him. Again, his subconscious cannot differentiate between the unnatural emotional bond with his mom and the more natural one with the other woman, it simply thinks all emotional bonds with a woman are bad.

Because the relationship will not mature normally, he also fears the other woman might leave him and therefore, he further attempts to manipulate, control, and abuse her in order to make the woman dependent on him so she cannot leave the relationship—the very essence of emotional abuse.

Whew! Get all that?

Therefore, four things combine to cripple the son during this type of abuse:

- The mother, needing her own emotional vacuum sealed, bonds with her son and steals any chance he has at forming a normal emotional relationship with another woman

- Subconsciously, he begins to hate all women because of what is happening to him at the hands of his mother

- He begins to control and manipulate in an attempt to prevent the other woman from gaining control over him (like his mother has)

- He subconsciously fears the other woman will leave him so he further abuses her in an attempt to make her totally dependent on him

I sat in class that night, totally transfixed on the television screen as the events of the last three decades of my life methodically played out before me like some fortuneteller with tarot cards. My chin rested in my hands because that was the only thing preventing my jaw from smacking the table.

I was not overwhelmed or emotional as I watched the presentation, because when you have the opportunity to sit in a movie theater and watch the private mysteries of your life be unpacked before your eyes, you simply sit there - as a wrung out sponge sits in a pool of water.

My father was my mother's life and there was a large emotional vacuum created in her when he died. In her pain, my mother reached out to me to have her emotional vacuum filled at the exact time I was preparing to find a girl that I could nurture, love, and provide for.

Believing I was "the man of the family," and it was my duty to provide for my mother, I reached back to her with an emotional lifeline. A bridge was formed between us and I was snagged hook, line and sinker into providing for my mom's emotional needs as well as her well-being.

A couple years later my mom, sister, and I moved back to my childhood hometown and it was not long before my eyes caught a neighbor girl who lived in the same condominium complex as me, walking home from school each day. Since I was a big-shot senior and she merely a sophomore, I didn't figure she was really my type so I didn't pay her much attention.

A few months later, I tried to help raise money for our school dance and I ended up going to this sophomore's condo. Her father answered the door and it turned out he graduated years ago from the same high school I attended in the small town from which we just moved. Since we both liked working on cars, he and I struck up a friendship. It wasn't long before I met that 'little' sophomore girl, Teri.

We messed around the next few years as simply neighborhood pals while she completed high school, though I must admit she had beautiful eyes and stunning legs. Just as I was about to leave for the Army we began to date and a couple years after I got out, we married.

Of course, we did not have a chance at any type of a normal relationship. I was whacked out thinking I had to provide for the well-being of my mother as well as dealing with the effects of being her surrogate husband and Teri had her own wounds from emotional, verbal and at times physical abuse from her mom.

She was codependent and I was a stinking, steaming pile of abuse waiting to happen. We were flat doomed in our relationship from day one and it's amazing things stayed together for as long as they did. I contribute that to the inner strength of Teri.

Snapshots into the Life of a Surrogate Husband

I was confused for many years during my teenage years and through my mid-20s when I married Teri. On one hand, I felt bad that my dad was not around to be with my mom, so I tried to do things to her help out, but on the other hand, when I graduated high school and started college, I was looking forward to what life had in store for me and was anxious to go live it.

I lived with this constant push—pull tug of war. I felt the push to be free and start my own life, yet I felt the constant pull from my mother. Even today, it is hard to discern when my desire to help my mom gave way to her emotional control of me. At any rate, from the time we moved the year following my dad's death, I don't remember a time when I was not at my mother's beck and call, or feeling guilty for not being so.

Here are a few snapshots I pulled from the memory banks today, showing what life as a surrogate husband was like for me. Fortunately, most of the memories have long been released from my mind, or erased.

I can remember one evening during my senior year of high school, I was getting ready to go out for the evening and my mother and I were arguing, something we did quite frequently during the push-pull cycles. My friend's girlfriend came to pick me up and as we were getting ready to leave, my mother said to me "If you go out that door and leave me, I don't know if I'll be alive when you get back."

I froze as my friend and I locked eyes in disbelief, an "Uhhh, did you hear what I think I heard" look on our faces. My friend said she would wait for me in the car as I sat on the steps leading upstairs and tried to figure out what the heck to do—I was all of seventeen-years-old. I knew if I caved to my mom's threat that I would be setting precedence and validating to her that that type of threat, of which I never heard before, was valid. Yet, I couldn't shake the thought that if I *did* go, would she go through with it and if so, how would I feel?

After several minutes, which felt like hours, I got up and told mom that I hoped she didn't do anything stupid and I would see her later. I walked out the door and went out with my friends.

Later, when I was on my way home, my stomach got more queasy the closer we got to my place—I had no idea what to expect. Since it was very late and my mom would normally be in bed with the light off, as soon as I came in the door, I flew upstairs and into her room and knelt close to her face to confirm she was still breathing... after which, I went to bed, my head still swimming from the night's earlier conversation with her.

The incident was never discussed following that evening (that Arrested Development thing in me), but there were several times during subsequent arguments when my mom made references to the evening and how - since I left in her time of need - I didn't really love or care what happened to her.

Several years after that incident, my mom requested I be sent home on a six month "Compassionate Leave" from the Army while she recovered from back surgery. I had no idea the Army had this type of leave and was mildly surprised to be sent home on one. During my time home, she pulled the same stunt on me following an argument. She was mad that I wasn't spending enough time with her and she told me the only reason why I was home and not back at my military assignment was because of her and her surgery. It must have been a bad argument because following it, I went to bed rather than going out or going to see Teri.

The next morning there was a several page suicide note waiting for me in my bathroom. I rushed into mom's bedroom to see if she were dead or alive and found her breathing normally. I checked her nightstand and all the medicine and kitchen cabinets to see if I could find any evidence of her trying to OD on pain pills or the like.

I was assigned to the local Army recruiting office while on leave and since calling off work in the military isn't an option, I faced quite a dilemma as to what to do. On one hand I was so angry with my mom that she would do this to me that I wanted to take her to the hospital and have her stomach pumped because that always sounded like a really nasty procedure to me. Perhaps it would tech her a lesson. Yet on the other hand, I saw absolutely no evidence she actually tried to kill herself, so right or wrong, I left and went to work.

Later on in the day, I called the house and she answered - she once again accused me of not giving a sh** what happened to her.

There were hundreds of times while I lived at home that mom tried to manipulate and control me, in her attempts to get me to stay with her rather than go and be with Teri. These attempts normally involved mom telling me in some form or fashion and said with the appropriate tears and low, crackling voice, how I either didn't love her or wasn't a good son if I didn't stick around.

I would think most mothers would understand that their son wanted to spend time with his girlfriend. I mean, while I was home to take care of her those six months, as long as she *was* taken care of and comfortable for the evening, it would certainly seem okay to me if I was down at Teri's house for a few hours. She only lived thirty yards away.

Many times it would be okay with mom if I did just that, but other times, she got very angry with me for even bringing it up and the thought of leaving her 'all alone'. I never knew which 'mom' I would get.

For some reason mom thought she had the right to speak her mind however she wanted, to whomever she wanted, anytime she wanted to. She would tell me that it was just her opinion and she was entitled to it. I would agree but remind her that just because she had an opinion, didn't mean she was entitled to speak it whenever and however she wanted to.

I don't think I ever won that debate in all the years I tried. The following is an example.

One year, Teri offered to drive the three hour round trip to bring mom to our house for a day or two. We hadn't seen her in about a year and thought it would be a little easier if she was with us in our home and surroundings, rather than being in hers. That way, we had plenty of room to 'get away' for a while if needed.

I was upstairs when my mom and Teri arrived at our house so I went down to say "Hi." As soon as mom saw me, the first thing out of her mouth was "Say there fatty." This was after not seeing me for a year! This is how you greet your son?

That one left a mark...

Mom became a very bitter woman after my dad died. She was so scared to let him go and move on with her life, so she didn't. If you didn't know my mom's situation and sat to have a talk with her, you would come to the conclusion that my dad was alive and merely away on some business trip or something. Even after he was gone, all her stories referenced 'we' not 'I'.

It is as if her mind ceased to record events that occurred in her life after he passed on. She never reminisced about her life following his death, never had anything to say about it; no stories of something eventful that happened recently or several years prior; no stories of the grandkids, or friends, or current events in the news—nothing. The whole point of reference in her life was back to the time she and dad were together.

On that day my dad died, mom died too. And, it was as if she expected the whole world to die right along with her. It reminds me of a saying; *we have one of two directions to choose when adversity strikes - 'betterness' or bitterness* - mom chose the latter.

Over the years she slowly withdrew from the world and the dozens of friends she and my dad had while he was alive. Bitterness makes you an angry person, unable to have joy for anyone or anything else it seems, even your own children.

My sister, four years older than me, quickly left home and struck out on her own after dad died and was never around much. I can't say I blame her, she felt she never measured up to the standards my mom had for her.

Therefore, for 33 years mom was my responsibility alone. There weren't other family members around and she eventually alienated all but one of the few friends who stuck with her. As she got older, my mom never traveled and very rarely left the house.

She looked to me to be her caregiver and house keeper - I was the sole source of her emotional and financial well-being, her sustenance. It was a role I took on, sometimes begrudgingly, even through the years of building a family and life of my own. I guess the truth is though, it wasn't a life of my own.

Mom could not let me go either. She could not find a way to live her life and enjoy seeing her son live his and merely enjoy the times she was included in it. Instead, she kept the emotional hooks set deep within me and kept the line taut, many times cranking a round or two on the reel if she felt I might get away.

Though I knew in my heart, all those years, I was doing the best I could for her, somehow, I always felt that I could, no *should,* do a little bit more.

My mother never approved of my relationship with Teri nor did she ever approve of Teri truth be told. I realize as a parent many times a child's courting preferences are not met with the most joyous of smiles, but Teri never gave any reason for my mom to feel anything less than adoration for her.

Teri was a very compassionate person and cared very much for my mom's well-being, and was sensitive to mom being all alone; this despite her knowing how mom felt about her, not from my words mind you, but from her own experiences with mom.

Through it all, Teri would help my mom out if I was unavailable due to work constraints or I was traveling—or sometimes just to give me a break from having to deal with mom. She didn't mind cleaning, going to the store, taking my mom on errands or to the Doctor's if that's what it took to help. She was a wonderful daughter-in-law and was very giving towards my mom, even when she didn't feel like it.

My mom would always smile and thank Teri and be very cordial to her face but never miss an opportunity to put Teri down to me or drop little 'she's not the right one for you' verbal hints prior to Teri and I getting married. She consistently tried to persuade me from getting serious with Teri and at times, flat out told me Teri would never make me happy as my wife.

Of course, it was mom's way of trying to control and keep me pinned to her rather than moving on to a life of my own. However, it added another layer of complexity and stress on to mine and Teri's relationship, which because of my abuse and control issues, had its own share of ups, downs and strife.

To top it off, my mom did not care much for Teri's parents and her parents did not care much for my mom. It was a real Peyton Place the majority of years Teri and I were together, and we were always thrust into the middle of the fracas.

———————————————

Neither Teri nor I could see that the abuse, control, manipulation, and anger mom was exhibiting towards me was flowing through me and on to her. There were times Teri could obviously see my mother was trying to control and keep me for herself, but she was not able to peer inside my head and see just how severely my mother's emotional control and lock on me was messing me up.

There were so many times that I had mixed feelings about staying with my wife and family or going to be with mom to bail her out of some obvious concocted situation.

Mom would call and tell me she heard a noise coming from her car and wanted me to check it out. Other times, she had some issue in her house that needed my attention, or she couldn't figure out how to program her VCR for an upcoming show. Still other times, she needed something that she could not reach on the top shelf of the cabinet, or a light bulb needed changed and she couldn't get the bulb out of the lamp. Or she dropped something and could not pick it up due to her back, or she needed a few items at the grocery and was completely out of food. Her bedroom drapes did not seem to be working correctly and the sun was too bright, etc., etc..

Other times she would call "just to talk" and proceed to lay into me for the next forty-five minutes because I was not being a proper son to her.

As her life and her depression spiraled further and further out of control, and she fell deeper into the blackness of her own misery, she subconsciously tried everything she could think of to get me to rescue her. Inevitably, I would respond to the life commandment in my head and the emotional hooks in my soul and go to her, all the while resenting her with the utmost resentment that I could muster.

I hated what she was doing to me but had absolutely no idea that what she was doing was stealing any chance I had to make an emotional bond with the woman I loved and married. She was robbing us of any chance at a successful marriage and I had no clue it was occurring, until it was too late.

My mother died on an Easter Sunday, three days before my divorce with Teri became official.

There's irony in there somewhere, and perhaps one of these years I'll spend time to find it—or perhaps it doesn't really matter at all.

I thank God that He allowed me to view the mother/son videotape during my class prior to mom passing. The last day of her existence on earth, I was able to hold her hand, as she lay unconscious in the hospital bed, and forgive her from my heart.

I realized when she reached out to me for an emotional connection all those years ago, that she was simply fighting for her own survival.

Unpredictable thing, that survival instinct is.

She didn't know what those hooks would do to my life and me. No, the mom I remember long ago was much more loving than that, she would never intentionally harm me. She was hurting, she was scared, and she did the only thing she knew to do.

So I told her in those final hours we had together that I forgave her and was not mad at her anymore... I told her she could let it be and go be with dad.

That Easter Sunday, I let go of my mother, along with the pain, anguish, and suffering the last 33-years of knowing her brought upon me and my life.

For the first time in a long while, longer than I can remember, I had a peace as I walked to my car that afternoon following her death. I somehow felt 'lighter'; the weight of carrying that surrogate husband no longer sat upon my shoulders. I left him in that hospital room to die as well.

So long mom... no hard feelings.

(Thank you Father, for your many blessings you bestow at the exact moment we need them. You are awesome!)

Chapter 8
Teri, I am Sorry for...

The soul would have no rainbow had the eyes no tears. __John Vance Cheney

One afternoon I presented the list that follows to Teri. It was without fanfare or sticking around to see if she gave me some positive strokes or feedback. Nothing I did made this about ME other than the fact that merely writing this list and giving it to my wife, provided some healing for my heart.

Teri told me later every one of the items listed was a 'hurt' for her. I believe this provided a small bit of healing for her wounded heart as well. At least I hope so.

This list was completed in one sitting in about an hour's time. The words flowed from my mind through my fingertips in a never ending cascade.

I didn't set out to do this beforehand, it was spontaneous and I'm very thankful it happened. Verbally saying "I'm sorry" is good, but letting Teri know I was aware of my transgressions and willing to put them in writing was even better.

As I move further away from the man this list represents, it is very painful to know this was the way I acted at times. This list is a reminder of the hurt I caused, and I hope I never forget how bad I behaved. We are not to dwell on our past mistakes but that does not give us the right nor excuse to forget them, or try to sweep them under a current day rug.

This represents life with me over a 30-year period – more than 10,000 days. Many of those days were not easy for my wife and yet I realize this surely must be only a partial list.

Please note, I have changed some of the wording to protect identities and to keep the book rated at PG.

Though I realize most of these 184 items won't make sense to you, I ask you to read the list and then ask yourself what *your* list would contain. What are you sorry for? Regardless of your spouse or your circumstances.

I am not where I need to be, but I thank God I am not where I was!

Teri, I am sorry for...

- Yelling at you and making you get out of the car and walk when we had an argument about not spending enough time at my mom's while we were dating.
- Telling you I thought your butt was getting big, even in a joking manner.
- Making rude comments or sounds when you'd bend over.
- Making fun of you in front of others just to get a laugh.
- Throwing our alarm clock at the wall during an argument.
- Treating you as a subservient person.
- Never supporting your decisions.
- Making you move to a new house without considering your needs.
- Telling you, "She's fine hon." When our daughter fell off the swing set backwards.
- Trying to get a laugh by calling you an a**&^le when you went to all the trouble to give me a surprise birthday party.
- Always having to control every situation, we ever faced.
- Thinking you were intellectually inferior to me.
- Not respecting your mother more.

- Getting angry with you that one time because you didn't get the right car part when I had a car problem.

- Causing us to have to get rid of our dogs when we moved from that new house.

- Blaming you for not speaking up about you not wanting me to buy the business.

- Giving you an ultimatum to have sex with me in order for me to marry you.

- Forcing you into pre-marital sex.

- Making you feel guilty because you did not want to lend me $400 to buy the TRS-80 computer many years ago.

- Using anger as a tool to get what I wanted, no matter the cost to you.

- Going to my cave for days or weeks on end.

- When I went to my cave not talking to you as a way to punish you. I knew it hurt you tremendously.

- Telling you how to dress as if you where my piece of property that I could use to display any way I wanted.

- Not appreciating every meal you worked hard to prepare for me.

- Yelling at you when you felt bad about something and I couldn't control you.

- Being an arrogant jerk.

- Learning to be a master manipulator of you.

- Thinking I knew you like a book so I could become a master manipulator.

- Ripping open all our wedding cards without recording the names and dollar amounts so we could send proper Thank You cards.

- Never helping you send out those Thank You cards.

- Not helping much around the house.

- Treating you as a sex object.

- Putting my mother first in our relationship more times than I can possibly remember.

- Thinking "our problems" were because of you.

- Not being more financially responsible about saving money and our future.

- Quitting my jobs without sitting down and valuing your input.

- Not recognizing you are my wise council.

- Not realizing that the majority of times, your decisions would have been right and mine were wrong.

- Never being able to say I was wrong for so, so many years.

- Forcing you to take diving lessons for my pleasure, not yours.

- Me being more interested in the baseball game than the birth of our daughter.

- The "Me Tarzan, you Jane" mentality I have had for the majority of our marriage.

- Taking your clothes and giving them to goodwill when I got mad at you.

- Not giving you the dream marriage, you had hoped for .

- Not being the man you thought I'd be and the one I fooled you into thinking I was.

- I am sorry that I ever stopped buying you jewelry to show off your beauty.

- Thinking I could read your mind.

- Thinking that I always knew what was best for you.

- Not bringing God into our marriage and becoming a godly man.

- Treating you terribly most of the time.

- Getting mad and yelling at you when you made the comment that "Men are idiots" one night while out.

- Getting mad and yelling at you when you made fun of me during our trip to Hawaii.

- Allowing my feelings to get hurt so easily and so many times.

- Not recognizing that I had anger, control and manipulation problems earlier and getting help.

- Not realizing just how important you are to me.

- Getting on my knees and begging to get our dog.

- All the times I simply would not "let it go" and accept "No" from you.

- Always having to have my way.

- Scolding you.

- Putting you down in front of the kids.

- Yelling first and thinking about it second.

- Never validating your feelings.

- Emotionally abusing you for our entire relationship.

- Adding guilt onto you to get my way.

- Never being able to hold down a job for very long.

- Not being able to respect authority.

- Not being a better parent when we first had the girls.

- I am sorry that I had so many ways to "make money" and make you suffer financially for my idiocy.

- Parking and watching you in the house last week.
- Convincing you to buy the boat when you didn't want to.
- Not trusting you.
- Yelling at the kids in order to control them.
- Putting you down in front of the kids.
- Always having the idea of "live for today and forget about tomorrow."
- Always trying to push my ideals, ideas and dreams onto you.
- Causing you embarrassment.
- Not listening to you.
- Not respecting how smart you are.
- Always putting my needs and wants before yours, making you feel that you were simply a "tag along."
- Not giving you security during our marriage.
- Not doing what needed to be done to build trust in me.
- Not buying you flowers more often.
- Not telling you "I love you" at least 5 times a day.
- Not being more tender and compassionate towards you.
- Not respecting your family more.
- The past 15 years being a living nightmare for you.
- Not making our marriage fun.
- Telling you to "^*&%-off" and "get lost!" when I was mad at you.
- Making you feel like you had to walk on eggshells around me.
- Not recognizing the signs of an abuser and getting help years ago.

- My Jekyll/Hyde personality - being "double minded" as the Bible calls it.

- Putting you down in front of your family.

- Putting you down in front of our friends.

- Failing this marriage.

- Making you feel like it was always your fault.

- Not taking you on more vacations.

- Not living up to my promises.

- Rolling that log and making you fall on your back when we went camping that time, just to get a laugh.

- All the times I knew you were hurting inside and I got mad at you because I did not know what to do.

- Not respecting you as my equal.

- Turning out like my mother and yet denying it all those years.

- Talking you into buying me a subscription to men's magazines so I could lust after other women.

- Never learning how to have a true (heart) intimate relationship with you.

- Not holding your hand more.

- Not appreciating just how hard you've worked at this marriage.

- Backing you so many times into a corner so you would apologize to me.

- Not recognizing every time you sacrificed yourself for me or the kids.

- The anger.

- Messing your life up.

- Thinking I was serving you while all the while, I was serving myself.
- All the times I preached to you as if I had a clue.
- Not being sensitive to your feelings.
- Saying you are the most selfish person I knew when you told me you wanted a divorce.
- Always controlling the finances.
- Using God to support my side and knock down your side.
- Never wanting to do what you wanted to do.
- Not being more spontaneous.
- Always making you feel dumb.
- Not learning to pray with you nightly.
- Not learning to just listen to you and not try to offer ways to fix it.
- Thinking you were less than me because you are a woman.
- Not respecting your privacy.
- Getting mad at you when you didn't come home when I thought you should.
- Insulting your intelligence.
- Not making you feel special and appreciated.
- All the times I continued to do things when you asked me to stop.
- Using the silent treatment to get what I wanted.
- Choosing to ignore you until you said you were sorry when we had a fight.
- Expecting sex whenever I wanted it but not giving it when you did.

- Not meeting your emotional needs and driving you to get them from another man.

- Not recognizing just how strong of a person you are.

- Making you wear a bathing suit when you were pregnant so I could make fun of you.

- All the times that I didn't do things around the house because I knew you would do them.

- Not doing more upkeep on our house.

- Having so many hobbies and interest and not simply appreciating you, the kids, our home, and our life.

- Always finding something to criticize about you.

- Not nurturing you.

- Not building you up but always tearing you down.

- Not complimenting you more.

- Taking you for granted.

- Not taking care of my body more to give you something pleasing to look at.

- Not letting go.

- All the emails.

- Expecting my needs to be the first priority of the family because I was the head of the household.

- Not knowing the true meaning of being the head of the household.

- Not reading more with you.

- Getting mad at you about something 3 or 4 times a week, maybe more.

- Not learning to enjoy your hobbies with you.

- Not working in the yard with you more.

- Interrupting you when you talk.
- Always acting like the victim.
- Limiting your spending money by giving you an allowance.
- Being unhappy so many days of my life.
- Ingraining in you and the kids "Is dad mad?"
- Getting mad and not staying overnight at the marriage seminar a few years ago.
- All the 1000's of more times I'm not remembering of "being mad because _____."
- Yelling at you 1000's of times.
- Not providing the means for you to fix up the house the way you wanted to.
- Destroying your dreams.
- Always having to struggle for money.
- Not going to kids events with you.
- Defending myself whenever you'd point out something I was doing to upset you or the kids.
- You being married to a man who was still a child in his emotional development.
- Not recognizing how hurt you were.
- Being verbally abusive.
- Taking my misery out on you and the kids.
- My ego and my pride.
- Putting you first instead of God.
- Making you feel as if you never measured up.
- Crushing the tender flower in you.
- Not building the children up spiritually.

- Always thinking your issues were "no big deal."

- All the tax problems.

- Not paying all our bills.

- Being lazy.

- Thinking I always had all the answers.

- Never apologizing.

- Never backing down.

- Telling you why you shouldn't feel the way you felt about things.

- Not learning the true meaning of a godly man and godly marriage.

- Having to make you suffer because of my fear of abandonment.

- Asking you to do things during sex that you didn't like or were not comfortable doing.

- Any event(s) that are strong in your mind that I have failed to recognize in this list that was ever hurtful, disrespectful or disappointing to you.

- Making you have to divorce me. There was no other way for me to wake up and realize exactly the person I have been and how I was in our marriage. I am waking up.

Poem
A Night in September

When a man has no design but to speak plain truth, he may say a great deal in a very narrow compass. __Steel

What follows is an entry I made on a blog created years ago to record my journey from the depths of my emotionally abusive behavior, in the hopes it might help someone else.

Since the blog was taken down and resurrected as the core content and motivation for this book, I decided to leave this in only for completeness sake, and not because it's important to the overall story.

I've never written a poem in my life. That may be obvious soon enough, but after spending several hours with my wife at our high school's football game one night, my heart was moved to put these words to paper and later, give them to her.

Doubt if they mean much to anyone but me, but felt I wanted to share as I close out this section of the book about our story.

I can't express the pain, knowing I've hurt the one I love so much, so deeply, all because of a wounding passed on to me when I was yet a child—it's a pain that resonates deep within my heart, never quite leaving me be.

It took me a long while to wake up from my nightmare, face the truth, and the errors of my ways... and realize just how much I have wounded others. I have no one to blame but myself.

Somehow, I hope there is healing in these words, they felt good to write...

A Night in September

seeing you tonight-
your doe eyes, your chestnut hair,
how I long to touch you,
how I long to share.
"I love you"

just sitting near to you,
I crave to kiss your face,
smell your skin,
praying to God for grace.
"I'm so sorry"

seeing your lips, your sensuous neck,
can't recall the last night we shared,
hearing your laugh and your giggle,
what I'd give for a marriage repaired.
"I was wrong"

knowing you need to grow,
my deeds and words hurt your soul,
wondering what's in your heart,
believing you're still not whole.
"please forgive me"

oh, when we shared that hug,
I know there's no guarantee,
but for that brief few seconds,
it was still just you and me.

things
learned

Chapter 9
Abuse 101

"Knowledge," says Bacon "is power," but mere knowledge is not power; it is only possibility. Action is power; and its highest manifestation is when it is directed by knowledge. __T.W. Palmer

It has been a little over five years since that Monday morning when I was set on the path to freedom from my abusive behaviors. As I continue on my journey toward better mental and emotional health, I occasionally encounter situations that in the past, would have unleashed that evil puppeteer within me and I would once again find myself under powerless control at the end of his strings.

My daily anger is a thing of the past and so is the need to control and/or manipulate my surrounds in order to protect that inner-child who years ago resided within me.

I signed up and attended the Life Skills program (more on that later) for a second six-month stint for a total of approximately 150 hours of training dealing with family dynamics and emotional abuse. Those weekly, three-hour classes were like water to my thirsty, parched soul as I drank up the teachings that pertained to my situations. I dearly wish the classes were offered in my current hometown so I could take a refresher.

As I mentioned previously, I spent the past five years working closely with a man who is emotionally and verbally abusive. His controlling, manipulative, and hostile ways were like a mirror reflecting back to me the man I used to be.

Our relationship ended recently when the company he owned was forced out of business. If I'm being totally honest, however, our relationship *nearly* ended several times over the years, as I fought the urge to beat him senseless about the face and neck with a computer keyboard during any one of his many tirades directed at unsuspecting and unarmed employees, vendors, or his wife, who worked there as well.

Alas, I am happy to report the fuse within me never ignited though many-a-match was held to the wick. It was a good test working in that oppressive environment and numerous times, as I sat there watching him abuse, I would think *That was me.*

A few times over the years working there, I slipped-up and resorted back to a form of the old-self, but I was fortunate that the awareness mechanisms now wired within my brain functioned correctly, and quickly shut down the behavior so I could calm down or take a time out, or both.

I had fits of anger for sure, but nothing that approached abuse or an intent to degrade anyone else. I suppose those moments were a reminder that although most of my former buttons and behaviors have vanished, some remain, and I suspect, *may* remain for quite a while.

I don't want to set up my own life commandment and say 'forever' but I don't think it's unreasonable, being only five years removed from three decades of abusive behavior, that I will have a few lingering affects linger longer than I'd like.

To you who think you see a form of yourself in the pages of this book but are inclined to discount your behavior or think you don't have a problem because your behavior is 'not that bad' compared to mine, please remember, I have condensed into only a few pages, the low points of abuse spread out over a 30-year period of time. I dare say the times Teri and I spent together were not all bad.

Moreover, the mere fact you are comparing your behavior with mine speaks volumes does it not? If you see *any* form of yourself in what I have written, I first commend you for being honest with yourself, and second say, "Beware my friend." At a minimum, you have some serious red flags that need to be looked at further.

Perhaps what follows will give you additional help and hope beyond what you've already read. Do NOT believe anyone who says someone who is abusive is incurable – that is NOT true. Emotional abuse *can* be stopped with the right care, the right education and most importantly, the right attitude. Having a teachable spirit is the key.

Please note, there is not a lot of information available on emotional abuse and I certainly am not a psychologist, counselor or psychotherapist. I hold no formal degree in any of what I am about to discuss other than a 30-year Degree of Life in 'Been-There-Done-That'. Personally, I think at times that is more valuable, but I would not encourage anyone to get the same degree I did.

I will share, as I've done throughout this book: *my* experiences and the things *I've* learned. It's not information gleaned from years of formal classroom instruction or years of experience gained from the treatment of others true. I feel confident, however, that what I present here is as correct as any other *credible* information available on the subject of emotional abuse, much of it from authors who have many credentials after their name. So keep in mind, the views discussed are from a single vantage point only—mine.

Because of my limitations of education in the abuse or domestic violence arenas, I cannot delve too deeply into much detail within any of the particular areas I'll discuss - I'll just hit the high points.

It was never the intention of this book to be a complete treatise on emotional abuse. If I've presented something perhaps you didn't know before, than I've educated and consider my job complete - I've accomplished what I set out to do.

If you recognize any of the same behavioral patterns I had in yourself or loved ones, I recommend you seek help or advice from professionals who are qualified and have specific experience in emotional abuse or domestic violence. Moreover, do it quickly - this *will not* go away on its own.

What is Emotional Abuse?

Plug that question into your favorite search engine and you will get as many different answers as there are websites. I found fourteen different definitions in under a minute.

Here is the one I use:

Emotional abuse is the act of belittling, ignoring, corrupting, and acting cruel, isolating, rejecting, or scaring another person, in an attempt to exert power or control over them.

The bottom line - anything said or done that attempts to *gain control* over another person is emotional abuse.

Emotional abuse touches all lifestyles and crosses all socioeconomic, ethnic, racial, educational, age and religious backgrounds. It is any behavior that is designed to control and subjugate another human being using fear, humiliation, or verbal assaults.

Emotional abuse is any kind of abuse that is psychological rather than physical in nature. It can include anything from verbal abuse and constant criticism to more subtle tactics, such as intimidation, manipulation, and refusal of the abuser to ever be satisfied.

Emotional abuse is akin to brain washing in that it systematically wears away at the victim's self-confidence, sense of self-worth, trust in his or her own perceptions, and self-concept. Whether it is done by constant berating and belittling, by intimidation, or under the guise of 'guidance', 'teaching', or 'advice', the results are similar.

Eventually, the recipient of the abuse loses all sense of self and remnants of personal value. Emotional abuse cuts to the very core of a person, creating scars that may be far deeper and more lasting than physical ones.

Types of Abuse

Most people are aware of emotional, verbal and physical abuse but there are actually twenty different types of abuse that can be used by someone to try to gain control or exert power over another person.

Any of these may be grouped together or a form of one may be extracted by itself. For instance, when I look at the list, I would have to categorize myself as verbally abusing Teri from time to time.

However, I wouldn't consider myself a strict 'verbal abuser' because I never exhibited the main, underlying traits used to define that type of abuse such as cursing or swearing at her or degraded her using names, etc.

I was able to identify twelve different forms of abuse that I used from time to time during my 30-years of abuse.

Physical Abuse

Striking, pushing, biting, choking, grabbing, shoving, slapping, beating or any other violent physical act against someone's will

Power

Denying basic rights; limiting someone's personal life; using the law to enforce power; controlling everything i.e., what lights to turn on/off in the house

Stalking

Spying or following someone; monitoring activities

Male Privilege

"Me Tarzan you Jane" attitude; treats victim as subservient; entitled to make all decisions

Knowledge Abuse

Uses knowledge from seminars, self-help books or therapy to abuse but does not take responsibility for own actions

Sexual Abuse

Demands usual sex acts; treats partner as a sex object; physical fixation or attacks to sexual parts of body; forces sex anytime day or night, even awakens partner for sex

Humiliation

Hostile humor; public humiliation; criticizes; degrades another on appearance, cleaning skills, cooking skills, appearance

Responsibility Abuse

Makes partner responsible for everything – paying bills, cleaning, cooking, parenting, etc.

Medical Abuse

Refuses to allow medical treatment for normal health issues or following a physical attack

Religious Abuse

Uses scripture with words like "obey" or "submit" to gain control

Using Children

Placing children in the middle to pass messages or gain information from; uses child support as a weapon to gain leverage; uses visitation rights to harass, etc.

Isolation

Requires victim to stay at home; limits time on phone; deprivation of friends; controls who is seen and when; restricts outside interests

Emotional Abuse

Puts another down; name calling; plays mind games; extreme controlling behaviors; withholds affection; causing one to lose their identity

Threats

Threatens ending relationship; threatens physical harm; threatens to take children away; threatens suicide

Economic Abuse

Gives allowance while controlling the money another earns, restricts employment; must account for all money spent; forces someone else to ask for money

Financial Abuse

Ruins partner's credit; requires cars, houses or recreational property to be in their own name yet uses partner's money

Intimidation

Uses looks, actions, gestures and voice to cause fear; argues continuously

Property Violence

Destroys property; punches walls; breaks down doors, etc.

Verbal Abuse

Curses, name-calls, use past to control or manipulate; makes unreasonable demands

Silence

Does not communicate; uses silence as a weapon; does not express emotion

Red Flags of Abuse

All forms of abuse are devastating and destroy individuals and their relationships. Here are some warning signs to look for. If you see a pattern of one or more of these behaviors in your mate, you could be a victim of abuse.

I was able to identify with seventeen of these twenty-nine flags.

Red flags of abuse

- There is blaming, cursing, or name calling
- One person controls the finances
- There is control of outside interests and friendships
- I see a 'Jekyll/Hyde' personality
- I make excuses for their behavior
- Sex is not always by 'mutual' agreement
- Household responsibilities are not shared
- There was violence or abuse in our families while growing up
- There are mind games, hostile humor, and/or put downs in public
- I cannot express my own opinion
- I have trouble communicating
- I live in fear

- I have unrealistic expectations for myself and others

- I feel isolated from my friends and family

- One person makes all the decisions

- I feel intimidated by looks, actions, and/or voice tone

- They threaten suicide or to leave me

- There is undue jealousy of my friends, family, and/or my time

- There is destruction of my personal property and/or abuse of pets

- My children are being used against me in any way possible

- I feel angry, on edge, depressed, trapped, and/or suicidal

- I find myself yelling at others, especially those I love

- I have been a victim of verbal, sexual, and/or physical abuse

- I feel alone with absolutely no one to confide in

- I struggle with feeling rejected

- There is no respect for privacy in our home

- Whenever I share things, it's eventually used against me

- I am constantly guessing what is wrong or what I did

- My partner/friend seems to tune me out and never really communicates with me

Chapter 10
Awareness

Awareness requires a rupture with the world we take for granted; then old categories of experience are called into question and revised. _Zuboff

Two things are key to breaking free and recovering from years of abusive behavior. These two keys go hand-in-hand with each other and are used daily, as we break free from abuse. Without them, I do not believe it's possible to begin or continue on the road to recovery from abuse.

The keys are *awareness* and being teachable, what I call having a *teachable spirit*.   I will look at awareness now and having a teachable spirit in the next chapter.

You cannot deal with something until you are aware of it. I said several times throughout this book that I had *no clue* I was behaving abusively the entire 30-years that I was. I knew some of the things I did hurt Teri, hurt her tremendously, but never once did I link up any of my behaviors with any form of abuse, nor did any of my friends or the five marriage counselors Teri and I went to over the course of our marriage.

I certainly wasn't proud of some of the ways I behaved, nor did I particularly like being angry about something nearly every day of my life. I believed, however, my behaviors were simply part of my character makeup, not a major brokenness within me. I would use terms like I'm *passionate*, or *I wear my heart on my sleeve*, or *I'm just emotional*, to describe my nature and excuse the way I behaved.

I never had a role model as far as what a good marriage should look like, or to show me how a husband should treat his wife. I thought the way I acted and argued with Teri was just the way couples interacted or argued. If we were in the middle of an argument and she said something to hurt me, I thought it was my married right to hurt her back, the *all's fair in love and war* mentality.

In addition, I couldn't help it if I was better at hurting her than she was at hurting me. After all, I reasoned in my sickness, she *did* make most of the mistakes in our relationship and because of her admitted co-dependence, had the most issues to deal with and fix.

All those years I calmly and rationally justified my behavior all the while shifting the blame and my focus to Teri. Never could I accept much responsibility for the issues in our marriage.

Once I had my *light bulb moment* and my eyes were opened to the truth, everything changed in an instant...

I became aware!

As I progressed through my journey to a healthy mindset, I realized there are three different levels of awareness we are given to aid in our recovery. I call these three levels, *who, did,* and *do:* the awareness of *who I was,* the awareness of *what I did,* and the awareness of what *I am about to do:* who-did-do. Catchy, huh?

Awareness of Who

The first level, the *Awareness of Who* is the ability to face the truth of the *who* we have become—we are someone with abusive behaviors. I believe this level of awareness is planted within us the moment we have our *light bulb moment.*

No longer could I deny the truth of *who I was*. From that moment on, I had a conscious choice to make every day - remain abusive or change. I was very aware of my abuse. I could no longer justify it, hide it under a rock or behind the mask I wore when around other people. I could no longer shift the blame to Teri. It no longer became the way Teri and I 'did marriage', it became a severe problem. Moreover, the problem was ME!

Notice I used the word 'was' and not 'am' in the first sentence above. It is important not to label oneself in the current tense as abusive, as in: I *am* an abusive person, or I am abusive, or I am an abuser. Instead use, I *was* an abusive person or I *was* emotionally abusive. We must try never to use the label of *abuse* in the current tense, or the *here and now* when referring to ourselves.

With my *Awareness of Who*, I consciously began to ask myself if there were any controlling or abusive motives in everything I said or did. Most times this was not an issue, because the desire to control and manipulate was not within me any longer. However, it took a while to get comfortable with my new self.

I was cautious to double-check my motives when interacting with others, at least initially. Many times, we will say or do things that we think are perfectly fine, only to realize later that there was a hidden motive to try and control the outcome of a situation, or perhaps control a conversation. I wanted no part of control in my life, not from an abusive perspective anyway.

I was very quick to clarify if I felt there was even a hint the other person may perceive what I said or did as manipulation. I probably took this to an extreme level in many cases, but I was not going to take any chances for manipulation to creep back into my life. I realized that whatever caused my brokenness and abusive behavior was still within me, so until I discovered the root cause of my behavior, I remained very cautious and aware of my daily conversations and actions.

I began to question *everything* about myself. I went to a new level of insecurity. I didn't trust anything about myself because every fiber in my body used to be programmed to control my world to protect my inner-child. At times, having this new awareness was not a fun time.

Eventually I learned a balance and realized no matter how much I wanted to, I was not going to be perfect. I *would* make mistakes. When I did, I had to learn to give myself grace and reassure myself that it did not mean I was falling back to where I came from, still trapped in my abusive ways.

I had to remind myself that slipping up from time to time just meant I was normal. I also discovered a second level of awareness I had - what I call my *Awareness of Did*.

Awareness of Did

As we former abusers interact with others, occasionally we will slip into old patterns of abuse and behave as we once *did*. The *Awareness of Did* brings these behaviors to our attention so we can address the matter quickly. It guards our current behavior, attitude and motives. It is our daily check and balance system to make sure we are moving away from whom we were and moving closer to who we will become.

Breaking free of the psychological pattern of abuse involves cutting the wires in the brain that lead to old, destructive circuits and rewiring them to new, healthy circuits. As much as I despise anything within me that has to do with abuse, I have come to realize some of that old wiring and circuits are still intact. It will take some effort and time to get it all rewired in my brain.

Until then, I have to trust that the systems now in place in my brain that keep me aware of my behavior throughout each day - my *Awareness of Did* - are working as they should.

I'm sure there are a few times during the past five years when I've slipped back to my old ways and been unaware, but 98% of the time when I say or do something hurtful without thinking, or allow a button of mine to be pushed, I become aware of what I did. Sometimes not immediately, it might take me several moments or several hours, but eventually I become aware. And the great news is, each time I do become aware, I am destroying the old circuits in my brain and building new ones.

Once I become aware of my behavior, I can go to the person I offended and apologize, or if going to them is not possible, say I was rude to a customer service rep on the phone, I can file my behavior away in my memory and hopefully not repeat the same behavior again. Each time I do this I build and fortify that new circuit in my mind!

It is not the setting of a new standard of perfection within us that's the key to our recovery, we'll *never* reach that level. It's an awareness of each time we make mistakes or slip up, and then being proactive as quickly as we can in repairing any damage done that is the key!

I have to tell you, going to someone, looking them in the eye and apologizing to them, without trying to justify our behavior is an amazing salve to hurt feelings or ruffled feathers. I am amazed at the reaction I get after I proactively apologize. The person almost has a shocked look on their face and many times, they are at a complete loss as far as what to say back to me.

I think being proactive and apologizing to our fellow man is becoming a lost art in today's society. We are so quick to blame others and justify our own behavior most times. I so enjoy being able to go to someone and humbly admit the errors of my ways, tell them I was wrong and apologize. I don't like the behavior that caused me to have to apologize, but there is such a cleansing I get after going to them that sometimes, I think I get more benefit out of the apology than they do! The more times I do it the easier it becomes.

I have freed myself from the standard of perfection and know that even though I will screw up many times going forward, I have the humility and tools (my *Awareness of Did*) to try and make right my wrongs. It is so *completely different* from the bondage I lived under before!

Awareness of Do

The third level of awareness is being aware *before* my behaviors turn nasty. I call this the *Awareness of Do,* as in, what am I about to do with my behavior and actions? This is the awareness I like the most. This one prevents me from having to apologize later for my actions or my words. Wahoo!

There are times when I become aware that a conversation or situation is headed down a path that may get my blood pressure elevated. In that moment, I can take corrective action to diffuse the situation, walk away, take a time out, or refuse to allow myself to get upset.

For me these are the golden moments in my recovery, I'm headed towards a potential conflict that in the past would have sent me over the edge and yet I handle myself *and* the situation as an adult. These are the times I know I am growing and getting healthier. I know that my brain is successfully getting rewired to much healthier circuits and I take yet another step on the road to recovery. YES!

I had a situation just a few months ago where my *Awareness of Do* kicked in big time. I was at the company where I used to work and I was having a conversation with the owner, who is emotionally abusive (I mentioned him in a previous chapter).

This man is used to imposing his will on just about any situation or person he comes across. He has an extremely short fuse and can become verbally abusive - cursing, name-calling, belittling - if things start to not go his way and he senses he is losing control of the situation or person.

We were having a conversation in front of the entire office and I mentioned something about a rumor I heard and wanted to call his attention to because it directly affected the conversation we were having. There were rumors flying all over the office because after fifteen years, the company was unexpectedly shutting down with very short notice—within days, we would all be without jobs.

The owner wanted to immediately know who I heard the rumor from instead of focusing on the current topic, which was the rumor as it pertained to our discussion. I knew he only wanted to find out the source of the rumor so he could go and unload an abusive tirade on the person. I held my ground and firmly, but professionally, stated that the *who* of the rumor didn't matter but the *what* of the rumor and our conversation did.

He could not get his focus away from finding out who passed the rumor on to me and he was beginning to impose his will on me by becoming verbally abusive in an attempt to find out. I took his verbal assault without becoming defensive or allowing my buttons to get pushed and finally told him clearly I would not reveal the source of the rumor because it had no bearing on our conversation and resolving the issue at hand.

I don't know if the owner finally realized that he was not going to get me upset, which really meant he was not going to be successful in getting me to relinquish *my* control to him, or if something else happened, but he stopped his personal attack on me and we continued the conversation a few moments later.

I felt very good about resolving the conflict and how I handled myself because the air in the office that day was very thick due to circumstances (closing the office down) and the owner was very volatile.

Later on one of my coworkers, who witnessed the whole confrontation, said she thought O*h boy... this is it... this is going to be World War III.*

My *Awareness of Do* helped me that day and it was a major hurdle for me to jump over and move forward. I was able to get into a major conflict with someone else who was trying their best to get me upset and get me to relinquish my level of self-control and composure (one of an abuser's tactics), yet I held firm and maintained a level of calmness. I didn't let his behavior influence my behavior or me, nor did I run away, unsure of how to handle the situation or myself.

After it was all over, I felt good.

With proper awareness, it is possible to relearn just about any learned, habitual pattern of behavior. I cannot tell you what it will take for the someone you know to wake up and become aware of their abusive behaviors, but once it does occur, I think you will see a breakthrough and a path opening towards healing and recovery that has not been there before.

There is hope! Hang in there!

Chapter 11
Being Teachable

I had six honest serving men —They taught me all I knew: Their names were Where and What and When —and Why and How and Who.
__Rudyard Kipling

Being teachable means, we are open to instruction and that we have a desire to listen, learn, and apply new things as we journey down the path to healthier behaviors and leave our abusive behaviors behind. There are many old, destructive ideas and beliefs we held during the time of our abuse that now must be replaced by new beliefs and new thoughts.

We will have to learn new ways to talk, new ways to listen, new ways to respond to others and to oneself, new ways to control our thinking rather than have it control us, and new ways to handle our anger, frustrations, insecurities, and fears.

There is lots of *new* to learn for sure!

The first step to all this new learning is to make sure we're open to learning it. It's easy to immediately say "Yes, I am ready to learn!" and that's good, however, when the ugly truth begins catching up to us and we're faced with having to look into that truth and admit some hard facts about ourselves, that's where the rubber meets the road.

We must be open to facing the truth about ourselves and have a willingness to be taught the things that are necessary for us to fully recover from our old patterns of behavior.

As I said in the previous chapter, being teachable and having awareness are both key to our recovery. We cannot have one without the other and be successful in breaking free of our abusive bondage.

If we have an awareness of the truth of our abuse and daily behaviors, yet are closed minded about learning new ways to guide us to healthier behaviors, we are not going to get very far in our journey to freedom.

Likewise, if we are open to being taught new things yet haven't developed our sense of awareness about our abuse and behavior, we will be equally hindered in our recovery.

When we open ourselves up to being teachable, what I call having a *teachable spirit*, we are coming from a place of humility and are saying, "I don't know it all, and I'm okay with that." We are opening ourselves up to new instruction and giving ourselves permission to learn from our mistakes and from the mistakes of others.

We come to a place where we realize our failures don't define who we are. We are also saying that it is not too late for us to learn new patterns of behavior, that we can improve no matter how bad things were in the past or how much damage we might have caused to ourselves or to others.

It took a while for me to develop my teachable spirit. I certainly had a desire to learn, but I was dealing with so many feelings and emotions initially that I had no idea where to start. Plus, I was dealing with quite a bit of shock and disbelief of coming to grips with what I was for all those years.

I didn't know if my abuse was fixable or whether I was going to be stuck in this hell for the rest of my life. I was experiencing so much pain, guilt, and shame that I had to allow those emotions and feelings to work through me for many weeks before I could open my mind to being taught anything new. I had to come to grips with the old first before I could move onto the new.

In hindsight, knowing that recovery from abuse is definitely possible, I still would have taken the time to process my initial shock, guilt, and shame, but I would have found some books or reliable information on the Internet to help me find a place to begin until I found more professional help.

I am not saying by merely reading good, reliable information on the subject of abuse and recovery that we can break free—we cannot. However, when we are faced with a mountain of adversity and we see no way over or around it, it is comforting to know others before us have faced the same adversity and negotiated it to a successful outcome.

Finding hope as quickly as possible, in whatever form it is found, gives us the inner resolve to continue.

What it means to be Teachable

So what does it mean exactly to be teachable and open to instruction?

- It means being open to other ideas, other than the ideas we currently have in our head

- It means being open to changing our opinion based on new information

- It means being able to admit when we are wrong, no matter the cost to us

- It means we are willing to ask questions in order to learn, even if it means our ignorance is exposed in the process

- It means we are willing to listen more than we are willing to talk

- It means we give up our right to act defensive when we are rebuked or criticized

Briefly, it means killing our pride and our ego and forcing ourselves back to a place of humility until we get all of the 'things' that we must relearn figured out.

I was diametrically opposed to every one of those bullet points above while I was held captive to my abuse. As I began my quest to get healthy, each one of those items was a hard, sometimes painful concept to internalize. I made more mistakes than I can count and I had many frustrations along the way, but my awareness came to the rescue.

My Awareness of Who kept me grounded and focused on my faults rather than everyone else's during those times when I wanted to shift blame. My Awareness of Who allowed me to accept correction from others and stay accountable.

When I wanted to give up and run away to the other side of forever, my awareness kept reminding me of my transgressions forced on the people I love the most. It gave me a new resolve to take one more step, to fail and fall once again, yet get back up one more time... to stay open minded to being taught and to learn.

Effects of Not Being Teachable

If we choose to not be teachable, we are saying we refuse to accept rebuke or criticism; that we refuse to learn no matter how many times we are presented with the same problems. We may find we have awareness of some of our abusive behaviors, but will always find some way to reason them away or blame someone or something else for the cause of that behavior.

Our pride tells us that we know what we are doing and don't need anyone else's help to recover.

I saw many men during the twelve months I was enrolled in my classes who would not allow themselves to be teachable. Perhaps they weren't fully aware of the depth or impact of their abuse. Perhaps they were of the mindset that "it's not that bad," which means they weren't willing to fully accept their responsibility.

More than likely, they incorrectly thought they could handle it on their own without anyone else's help. Their pride and ego kept them in bondage.

Whatever the reasons, they remained close-minded to the truth and refused to be taught what they so desperately needed to learn. I am sure it didn't take long after the six-month class was over for them to slip back into their old patterns of abuse.

There were a few times I wanted to go up, knock them upside the head, and yell "WAKE UP!" Nevertheless, it would have fallen on deaf ears. They had not hit bottom yet, and the pain of their miserable life had not become severe enough for them to want to change.

They refused to remain open to a total awareness of themselves and face the truth of who they were; that closed off their ability to be teachable. Their inner child was fearful and they chose to isolate themselves to protect it and refused to grow up.

It was very frustrating and at times painful to watch because their freedom was right before them yet they could not take the steps necessary to gain it! Until they are ready to pay whatever price needs to be paid in order to be free, they will remain a prisoner to their abuse... and make some innocent victim pay for it.

Symptoms of an Unteachable Spirit

There are a few self-checks we can perform to gauge if we have parts of us that are unteachable.

- Are we are *being argumentative and/or defensive* about any area of our behavior, or our willingness to *accept criticism* from someone else, especially our partner?

- Are we willing to *accept responsibility* for our mistakes along the way, or do we instead look to blame others?

- Do we *isolate or withdrawal* when we run into challenging times. For instance, when our mate criticizes us for the way we just behaved, do we withdraw and perhaps go to our cave and justify our action by saying "Well, at least I didn't stay there and argue with her and try to justify my behavior."

- Are we are *holding ourselves accountable* to anyone else, or are we surrounding ourselves with people who will tend to agree with us?

There were many times when I had to stop and do these evaluations on myself or ask friends, whom I knew would be completely honest with me, to evaluate my behavior in these areas. Many times, I found myself doing well in some areas and not so well in others.

I would make a note in my journal about the areas that needed attention I would spend some time meditating on those issues and allow myself to receive honest answers, even if those answers were painful and not really what I wanted to hear.

I knew the problem existed within me and I knew I was fixable. I was willing to spend whatever time it took to get the answers I needed in order to get healthy. Many times, it would be months before I had a breakthrough... but eventually breakthrough I did!

These self-checks were also a time to evaluate if I was allowing pride and/or ego to creep back in to my life or, was I keeping myself in a place of total humility. Humility would probably be the third key I would list that is critical to recovery from abuse.

It might be helpful to have our partner evaluate us in the previous areas as well, and then compare their answers with ours. Keep in mind, whatever our mate wrote down or told us in response to their evaluation is the *correct answer,* regardless of what our answer is.

Three Ways to Learn

During my journey to recovery, I have come to understand that there are only three ways in which we learn:

- The *easy way* allows us to learn from the mistakes of others
- The *hard way* allows us to learn from our own mistakes
- The *tragic way* doesn't learn from the two ways above

Chapter 12
Arrested Development

Whole years of joy glide unperceived away, while sorrow counts the minutes as they pass. __Havard

Arrested Development is a condition where something traumatic happens during the childhood years that *lock* the emotional development of the child at whatever age the trauma occurred. The earlier the trauma, the earlier the emotional lock on the child. This normally dictates the severity of the abusive behavior—the earlier the lock the more violent the abusive behavior.

Psychologists may refer to Arrested Development as fixation. It is a nasty condition and is the *number one symptom* of someone trapped in abusive behavior I believe.

If you find yourself in an abusive situation, it is almost guaranteed some trauma occurred during the abuser's childhood, which froze their emotional development. The good news is—the effects of this condition *can* be stopped and the person affected *can* recover.

I did it (with loads of help) and others have done it too. There is hope and I want to encourage you as you read on.

Arrested development is a very complex subject. There is no way I can cover all the material in this single section, nor am I medically qualified to speak to all the nuances, twists and traps of the condition. However, it is important to grasp the *concept* of Arrested Development because left untreated, it will *continually* cripple us in our life and in our relationships as we progress physically into adulthood and adult responsibilities.

We CANNOT outgrow Arrested Development. It stays with us until we either face the cause of it and heal... or we die.

It is that simple.

Let me give you a brief example of Arrested Development as it pertained to my own life. My father died when I was fifteen. I was a late bloomer and an immature fifteen-year-old. Emotionally I would say I was around twelve years of age. I had not yet developed the necessary coping mechanisms to effectively handle my dad's sudden death. The trauma overwhelmed me.

My *emotional development* became locked yet my physical development continued. As the years progressed, I was an adult on the outside but inside, I was still a twelve-year-old child. I processed my surroundings and situations as a twelve-year-old rather than an adult; I handled anger, conflict, relationships, and emotional intimacy as if I was still twelve years of age! Of course, this led to huge problems as I grew up and married Teri.

Why Arrested Development Occurs

Research shows that young children under the approximate age of thirteen lack important chemicals (serotonin, dopamine, and norepinephrine), called neurotransmitters—think communication agents that interlink and move messages around our brain. These particular chemicals help us to think abstractly and process *the big picture,* which in turn helps us to make proper decisions as we mature emotionally.

Our Creator realized that before the age of thirteen we really do not have many decisions to make, at least not compared to adulthood, so there is little need for these chemicals to be released into the brain.

As we mature through puberty and progress from being dependent on our caregivers to independence, these chemical neurotransmitters are released into our brain in order to help us to think abstractly and make decisions on our own, we are taught boundaries and consequences to our decisions, both negative and positive.

With the proper operation of these neurotransmitters delivering messages throughout the brain, we learn to become a decision maker based on abstract thinking. We are set for the rest of our life.

However, if severe trauma happens to us in childhood, prior to when the *decision-making* chemicals are released into the brain, our emotional system locks forever and we will never develop the ability to think abstractly and make decisions as a normal adult.

Whatever age we were when the trauma occurs, pertaining to our emotional development, is where we will stay for the rest of our lives. Even though I was fifteen when my dad died, emotionally I was probably age twelve.

There are four broad categories of trauma that most commonly arrest the development of the child: rejection, sexual abuse (incest or molestation), emotional abuse, and physical abuse. Any one of these events, can arrest our development, or there may be a cluster of two or three events in a short period of time (such as the death of one or both parents) that can cause the arrest.

Characteristics of Someone With Arrested Development

If we are arrested in our development, we will continue to make childish decisions when faced with stressful situations. We have no control over our impulses and our relationships are impacted because we process everything with childish emotions and intentions.

A person arrested in their emotional development will normally be characterized by the following:

- immature
- unable to resolve issues
- rejects authority
- cannot limit themselves
- unhappy with their job
- unstable
- lacks impulse control
- searches for freedom

I had all of these characteristics!

Development Stages of Life

Erik Erickson did a study on the eight developmental stages of life from birth to maturity. For this discussion, let us look at the first six stages briefly to get a sense of how we grow emotionally, from birth through early adulthood.

The ages listed below are not absolutes as far as when the development *must* occur, but should be used as a general guide. If our emotional development gets locked at a particular stage due to our trauma, we will not be able to advance to any subsequent stages. This is why being exposed to trauma at an early age has such a devastating effect on us as we grow older.

Stage I – birth to 1 year old

If life cycle completes - child learns basic trust; a sense of order and stability – they cry (communicate) and their needs are met; they gain feelings of being loved, wanted and cared for. The successful lasting attribute of these cycles is drive and hope.

If life cycle does not complete – child learns basic mistrust; life is chaotic; child is sick physically and psychologically disabled; academics are severely impacted.

Stage II – 1 to 3 years old

If life cycle completes – child learns autonomy; to stand on their own two feet and feed self; controls bodily functions; makes needs known through language; discovers choices as well as "No" and "Yes"; learns the rules of society. The successful lasting attribute of this cycle is self-control and will power.

If life cycle does not complete – child learns shame and doubt; produces passive dependency on others; cannot assert own will; rebellious personality.

Stage III – 4 to 6 years old

If life cycle completes – child learns initiative; learns time and geography; can *go* and come back; can think in terms of future; has developed memory; more loving and secure in family —good chance to become a *moral* person. The successful lasting attribute of this cycle is direction and purpose.

If life cycle does not complete – child learns guilt; always wants to be in control; over competitive —may always be "outside" the law or rules.

Stage IV – 6 to 12 years old

If life cycle completes – child learns industry; the *how to* of society, masters the "3 Rs" and learns to feel worth and competence. The successful lasting attribute of this cycle is method and competence.

If life cycle does not complete – if child fails to learn industry, feels inferior compared to others; if child over learns industry, may become too task oriented and rigid.

Stage V – 12 to late teens or early adulthood

If life cycle completes – person learns identity; sexual identity; discovers role in life; begins to answer, "Who am I?" outside of family role; develops social friendships; begins to distance from family. The successful lasting attribute of this cycle is devotion and fidelity.

If life cycle does not complete – person learns confusion; may not develop own personality outside of family; may not become socially adult or sexually stable.

Stage VI – early adulthood

If life cycle completes – person learns intimacy; learns to share passions, interests and problems with another person; learns to think of *us, we,* or *our* instead of "I"; associates with work, family, and community; achieves stability. The successful lasting attribute of this cycle is association and love.

Impact of Arrested Development On Our Lives

It is important not to over analyze the life cycles above to try to *figure out* at what age our emotional development froze. Everyone develops at a different pace—I was fifteen when my dad died, but emotionally I was closer to a twelve-year-old.

The important point is to understand we develop in cycles and if trauma happens during one of these cycles, we *lock* emotionally to that level and never progress beyond it. The earlier the trauma, the earlier the development is arrested.

If our emotional growth is stopped, we do not have a chance to develop character in certain areas of our life. We never accomplish a way to cope with the pain of our early childhood trauma, yet as we grow older physically, we wear a mask to show the world *all is well*, sacrificing ourselves within.

As we age, we try to meet the expectations of another person or society but we only serve to sacrifice our own development. As a twelve-year-old child, I was never meant to satisfy the needs of another woman.

Arrested development will manifests itself in many negative ways as we try to function as an adult in important areas like:

- *anger management*
- *conflict resolution*
- *cooperation*
- *emotional intimacy*
- *financial management and accountability*
- *sexual development*
- *stability*
- *communication*
- *confidence*
- *compassion*
- *social skills*

Briefly, Arrested Development influences *every* area of our life and *every* relationship we try to form. The list above is only a *few* of the areas Arrested Development can manifest in an adult's life. I was crippled in every one of the areas listed!

Breaking Free from Arrested Development

As complex as Arrested Development is, breaking free from it is relatively simple—on paper anyway.

I again caution —this process is best left in the hands of a professional. What I am describing is an overview of what must be done in order to release ourselves from the grip of Arrested Development—to show it is a relatively straightforward process.

My goal is to give hope that there are steps we can make to become completely whole again, many times for the first time in our lives! I am not trying to give a self-help, self-heal clinic hear.

To free ourselves from the lock of Arrested Development, we must be willing to go back, revisit our earlier childhood traumas, and release them. We must tell ourselves that the trauma was not our fault and we were completely powerless to stop it—that we are not damaged and dirty because of the trauma.

It is okay as we revisit the trauma, if we 'tell' the offending person or persons how they made us feel and what that did to us, but ultimately, we must be willing to release them from the damage to ourselves. They were, after all, probably damaged during *their* childhood but never got healthy.

Your brain will fight you every step of the way during this process because it has built many mechanisms over the years to protect you from the trauma. It might take many attempts before you are able to break through and reach the traumatic event or events or, it might take a while before you can begin to remember them at all.

You may also experience physical reactions as you attempt to visit these areas of your childhood such as sweats, chills, tremors, or an overwhelming urge to run, as adrenaline releases and courses through your body.

Yes, there may be a heavy price to pay in revisiting painful areas of our childhood to break the grip of Arrested Development but it *must* be done in order to heal, grow up, and mature inside.

I can promise, however, *every* painful experience we allow to be brought forth in order to heal, will *forever* release its grip on us (and through us, our loved ones). We will be set free to function as the adult we are! For the first time in our life, we will start to like the person we have become.

It is a feeling that took me forty-eight years to feel and it is awesome! Go for it!

Chapter 13
No Excuses -
Accept Responsibility

Responsibility educates. __Wendell Phillips

Abusers are great at never accepting blame for the mistakes they make - the hurtful words they say, the destructive actions they take. They can play the victim very well and twist things around masterfully in order to come up with an excuse for their behavior— even when apologizing.

For example: "I'm sorry I yelled at you last night hon. I was upset when you got ready later than I thought and was nervous we wouldn't get a good seat for the movie. I didn't realize we would get there so quick. I could have handled it a lot better than I did. Sorry." Is this person apologizing for their behavior or justifying it? "Sorry" wrapped around an excuse is still an excuse.

We alone are responsible for our words and actions, regardless of what anybody else does or doesn't do, says or doesn't say. Yes, at times people can attempt to push our buttons, but ultimately, it's up to us to decide whether we allow them to do so or not.

During those times when we do allow our buttons to be pushed and respond in a less than desirable manner, we must accept our mistake and not look for others to blame. When we refuse to accept responsibility for our actions, we disassociate ourselves from our behavior that did the damage.

Our inner-child cannot handle accepting responsibility because it does not know how to deal with it.

Have you ever seen a child with chocolate syrup all of themselves yet deny they had anything to do with the chocolate syrup mess on the kitchen counter? They don't yet know how to accept the responsibility for what they did so they will stand there and do the only thing that they know how—deny it.

As an abuser, we do the same thing (though hopefully not as blatantly obvious as the child in my example).

When I began to take ownership of my own transgressions towards others, it was a great feeling to go to someone I wronged and apologize. "Sorry for _____. I was wrong. Please forgive me." That's it. No need to shift blame or try to *explain why* I said or did what was wrong. It felt GOOD to me to be able to do it.

Along with accepting responsibility, we must work to focus only on *our* transgressions and not those of our mate's. So many times, I would say to myself "Yes, I know I have issues, BUT if Teri would only _____ , then our marriage would be a lot better. Why can't she understand that?"

For years I honestly thought Teri was the one to blame for most of our marriage issues because I was the one reading the self-help books and suggesting seminars to go to or video tape series to watch, not Teri. I was completely blinded to the truth.

We CANNOT fix anyone else. We cannot convince, connive or cajole *anyone* into facing his or her own issues. Leaving articles or books lying about will not work. Sitting and watching a seminar or TV program that talks about *their* problems, hoping they will finally *get it* if they hear someone else talking about what is wrong with them is a waste of time.

We MUST focus only on ourselves. After all, we are the only ones *we* can fix. In addition, most of the time, if we fix our issues, the other persons issues will either disappear or won't seem to be as big of a deal to us as we first thought.

We will begin to operate in a place of grace and mercy towards others as we realize how many issues we have that we need others to give *us* grace and mercy for.

We are *all* broken people who need compassion, love, understanding, and grace. There is no better way to receive all those things than by first giving them away, without any expectation of getting them back.

Over time, those we love will start to feel *safe* around us and begin to open up and tell us things about our behavior that bothered them or hurt them because they know they are likely to get a simple "I'm sorry" in return, rather than a dissertation of why what we did or said wasn't our fault.

Accepting responsibility is a sign of maturity and a sign of leadership. Others will respond if we consistently do the right thing by owning our actions and words.

Chapter 14
Anger 101

Men often make up in wrath what they want in reason. __Alger

Anger is good. It is natural for us to have feelings of anger, they are not bad feelings that we should try to fight and suppress. It is what we do during those moments of anger that slowly shape our world.

Much of how we look at anger and how we process our thoughts and our surroundings when we're angry stems from our childhood. At a young age (typically 1-3 years old), as we began to try to shape our world, were we allowed expressing our anger in a healthy manner or were we told "Be quite!" or "Don't talk back!"?

Did our parents retaliate or abandon us during our fits of anger and rage or did they hang in there and allow us to vent or rage? It is during these early, impressionable years that we form life long, deeply rooted feelings about anger and its uses.

Where Does Our Anger Come From?

Our Creator gave us anger to alert us something is not right in our world. Could be something as simple as being angry because we are late for work and get caught at a traffic light. Our anger had one simple root cause – an unmet expectation we *expected* to be at work on time. However, our anger response to the traffic light was really due to a primary, underlying feeling.

ANGER IS ALWAYS A *SECONDARY* RESPONSE TO

AN UNDERLYING *PRIMARY* FEELING OR EMOTION

As an emotionally healthy adult, projecting anger at the traffic light may be a cue from our response to sit back and reflect for a few moments on our feelings, rather than take immediate action and normally say something we might later regret.

We might do a little self-reflecting about our approach and attitude about getting to work on time. Perhaps we are running late because we don't feel appreciated at our workplace or we have anxiety about how our boss or coworkers treat us. Not feeling appreciated may conjure up our feelings of insecurity from our childhood. We felt like we never measured up in our parent's eye because they never gave us positive feedback but always pointed out the negative.

We do not feel appreciate at our workplace because our boss does not tell us that we are doing a great job as much as we would like to hear. We feel that once again, we do not measure up. Nevertheless, when we think about it, we have gotten two raises in the past 18 months along with more responsibility. Though we don't get the audible *positive strokes* we'd like, the fact we are getting additional money as well as responsibility tells us we must be doing a good job.

Processing what is going on inside us when we get angry at something, a traffic light on the way to work for instance, is a much healthier way to use our anger. Do we control our feelings of anger, and use it for something constructive, or do we allow our anger to control us and *fly off the handle* in a rage, saying whatever comes to our mind and throw gasoline on an already burning fire?

Anger & Arrested Development

If we are an abuser and arrested in our development, we cannot process anger as a normal, healthy adult and use it for something constructive. There is no chance to sit back and reflect on our primary feeling or emotion because we never developed the capability to think abstractly or see *the big picture* due to our childhood trauma.

We are locked emotionally as a child inside and process anger just as a child would - by many times flying off the handle and speaking or acting first and thinking second. A child doesn't know how to get in touch with their underlying feelings of insecurity, anxiety, or rejection. They are simply mad that something in their world is not conforming to their perceptions of how their world should be— their expectations are not being met.

In my own life, I didn't know how to process my inner feelings about my father dying. The loss of my security knowing my dad would always be there, the deep hurt within my heart and soul over losing him, and the loss of family unity and cohesion that a mother and father bring to the table.

I also felt a sense of anger toward him for dying when I was young and stealing the opportunity I had to grow up and share father-son activities with him. There was anger because my father dying devastated our family and we never recovered from it. In some situations a parent dying at a young age brings a family closer together but in our case, it shattered it. My mother, sister and I never recovered as a family unit.

So I stuffed my feelings deep within and began to build my "I'm fine, I can handle it" mask. Yet, inside, my anger and resentment began to build.

Within a short period of time, my mother and I latched on to each other emotionally and as a result, my ability to emotionally connect with Teri and perhaps share, process or release those earlier feelings about my father dying were gone. Our relationship was based on a physical foundation not an emotional one.

As I continued to stuff the feelings of my dad's death further within, I also began to subconsciously resent what my mom was doing to me emotionally. As the surrogate husband role between her and I progressed over the years and her noose of control tightened around my life, I formed a *no woman will ever do this to me again* frame of reference within my mind.

Outside I was growing into a man but inside I didn't have a clue how to deal with my inner feelings and emotions nor did I possess the ability to handle conflict. Just as a child, all I knew how to do was *get mad* when things didn't happen the way I thought they should happen (which was all the time it seemed).

When we are arrested in our development, we do not have the necessary chemicals in our brain to process *the big picture* and get in touch with why we feel the way we do. Our inner-child only knows how to express itself, get what it wants, and try to control its external world by using one of two feelings—joy or anger. Up or down. It's a constant roller coaster of emotions for us suffering from Arrested Development. We are a scared and in a constant state of survival—a little kid in an adult world with adult responsibilities.

What an Abuser Gets from Anger

After Teri and I started dating, it did not take me long to realize my anger could be used to my advantage. I used it to manipulate and get what I wanted. It became a good friend to me, so I fed my anger and used it as a tool for my own personal gain, while gaining this false sense of belief I could control it. The truth was however, it soon controlled me.

As an abuser, there are many ways we use anger as a tool, depending on the situation or what we are feeling at the time. Here are some of the more frequent ways:

Shift blame

Anger allows us to blow out of proportion something minor our mate does, yet not taking any responsibility for something we did during the same time period. If we both messed up, anger allows us to easily shift the blame.

Cover weaknesses

We can cover our feelings of inadequacy, rejection, hurt, fear, anxiety, embarrassment, etc., all by using anger. We shift the focus to our anger and away from our weaknesses.

Receive attention

Sometimes, if I felt ignored around the house, I would ramp up my anger to get attention; much like a spoiled child who doesn't care what kind of attention they receive, good or bad, as long as everyone's attention is on them.

Feeling of strength and invincibility

We feel invincible and power can literally surge through our body as we became angry and take control of a situation. Other people back down from us and we feel as if we *command respect*. We feel as if we can conquer any situation that we face with the right amount and application of anger.

Keep others at a distance

If someone starts to get too close to our inner feelings we use anger to push them away. Anger helps keep others at a distance from us and the truth about what is going on inside us. Those feelings represent pain, and pain is to be avoided at all costs, even at someone else's expense.

Briefly, anger becomes the only survival mechanism we know how to use effectively.

The Hidden Cost of Our Anger

There is always a hidden cost to our anger. People will begin to avoid us for fear of being caught in our angry outburst. This often leads to a life of bitterness because we are lonely.

Trust is lost among those closest to us because it's hard to trust someone who is not in control of their anger. Without trust, vulnerability begins to subside because our mate must trust us before they are comfortable showing their most vulnerable side to us.

As trust and vulnerability leave the relationship, love begins to fade—taking feelings and intimacy along with it. Soon, as in my case, the entire relationship from our partner's viewpoint is meaningless and unless something changes quickly, the relationship could be doomed.

Our anger causes those around us to become afraid. No one knows when our angry tirades will start or how we might act once they do. Who in their right mind would want to hang around a bottle of nitroglycerin, when the least little *bump* could set off a huge explosion?

Many times our angry outburst causes others to seek revenge. There's a saying that *violence begets violence* and it's human nature to want to get even with someone who has *wronged us*. The other person doesn't necessarily have a conscious plot to get even with us but it may come out in an argument or our mates own hostile humor towards us.

Finally, our anger and violent outburst teaches our children to do the same. As our children grow up exposed to our anger they may begin to form their own misguided beliefs that if you're angry enough, big enough, are always right, and the other person is your mate, than it's okay to be angry.

The terminal costs of anger in an abusive relationship is as follows: normal problems progress in the marriage, bitterness builds within the abusive partner which leads to resentment of their partner; this in turn eventually leads to some type of abusive explosion, and the anger-abuse cycle repeats itself repeatedly over the years until the relationship is terminated. I have been there and done it. My hope is you will not follow my example.

Chapter 15
Triggers

When anger arises, think of the consequences. __Confucius

A trigger is a pre-conditioned response to a past event that is internalized within us. Something might be said or done to us and immediately, we respond with an angry outburst or become withdrawn and isolate ourselves. We might not know why we responded in the way that we did.

We may respond with a sudden emotional outburst or we may not be able to respond at all. We might be so fearful that we are instantly paralyzed and unable to move or say anything. We know something happened within us, but we might not have a clue what it was or what caused it. Before we knew it, we reacted.

If not dealt with, triggers can cripple us as we get older. Remember from the previous chapter on anger, that anger is always a *secondary response* to a *primary feeling*; anger is never primary, it's always secondary. There is *always* an underlying feeling to our response of anger.

Triggers are deeply rooted in our subconscious that take us back, normally to an event from our childhood, where we suffered some type of feeling towards a traumatic event or events in our life. They could be feelings of rejection, abandonment, emotional scars from abuse, inadequacies, or worthlessness to name a few.

Examples of a Trigger

Say for instance, my mother told me repeatedly when I was a child "You're worthless," or, "You'll never amount to anything." Hearing those degrading words from my mother, whom I thought would always love and nurture me, caused me to withdraw and isolate myself in my bedroom and tell myself how worthless I was. I felt meaningless and wondered why I was born, and I responded by withdrawing from the world and my miserable life.

Alternatively, let's say I was verbally abused as a child; my father continually yelled at me and beat me down with his words, telling me "You always make the wrong decision," and, "You are foolish, and worthless."

Though I was much too young and afraid to get into a confrontation with my father, I would walk to the woods behind our house, find a stick and proceed to beat a tree or anything I could find as hard and violently as I could, all the while raging as if the object were my father. I felt worthless and inadequate, and I responded in anger and unchecked rages towards the one making me feel that way.

In each of these examples, my feelings of worthlessness and inadequacies left deep emotional scars within me. My subconscious recorded each event along with my feelings in response to those events.

Fast-forward to today; Teri and I are discussing buying a lawnmower that I saw for a good deal. I thought it was a good decision to buy it and wanted to talk to her before I did. I was sure she would agree.

During the discussion, she says to me "I think you're being foolish for wanting to spend money on a new lawnmower when ours is working fine."

I have a trigger response and immediately lash out in an unsuspecting rage towards her, telling her how foolish I thought she was for buying those expensive bed coverings a couple months ago when we already some.   Before I know it, a full-blown argument ensues. What started out as a discussion over spending money soon becomes a wedge driven deeper into our marriage.

My trigger was my subconscious taking me back to the time my father verbally abused me along with my angry response to the feeling of worthlessness I had. My mind caused me to respond to my current feelings of worthlessness just as it did the last time I felt the same way—rage and anger.

A circuit in my brain has been formed between my feeling of worthlessness and the angry response to that feeling. This circuit is reinforced the more times it is triggered and soon becomes my automatic response to my feelings of being inadequate or worthless.

Though Teri was correct in telling me I was foolish for spending money we didn't have, on something we didn't need, my perception of her words were she was my father verbally degrading me and I responded to her with the same rage and anger that I did back when I was a child.

Actually saying my subconscious took me "back to a previous time" is not quite correct. Our subconscious records the events in our lives but it is not capable of differentiating between the past and the present. It merely knows that an event and feeling I am experiencing now matches the same event/feeling in its memory bank.

Sometimes we might not trigger an angry response to a situation, but rather withdraw and isolate ourselves. It all depends on what our feelings and responses were to that initial trauma during our childhood.

Let's use the example above of my mother telling me I was worthless, causing me to isolate and withdrawal, and apply it to the same scenario of the lawnmower discussion.

If the outcome of the discussion causes me to withdrawal and isolate myself, I may allow bitterness and resentment toward Teri build within me for a period of days and even weeks. Eventually that bitterness and resentment will come out of me in some form of anger. I might explode over a relatively minor issue weeks down the road or I might go through a period of weeks and use hostile humor to degrade her whenever we are around friends or family.

In both of these examples, I cannot handle the situation like an adult and work towards a win – win solution that would build trust and intimacy in our marriage. Since I am arrested in my development and handled the discussion as a child would, I caused our marriage to break down further.

A less obvious but equally destructive example of a trigger response to my feelings of worthlessness would be this: I am super excited to give Teri her birthday gift, a new outfit, because I think, she will love it and look dynamite wearing it. Immediately after opening the gift, I can tell she doesn't really like it even though she is trying not to hurt my feelings by telling me so.

Instead of telling her it's okay if she doesn't like it and that I'd love to go with her as she tries on some different outfits, as long as she promises to model each one for me, I feel an anger well up inside me. I am not good at hiding my feelings, so Teri notices my projection of anger and this leads to an underlying tension between us that will fester and more than likely blow up sometime in the future.

Once again, my trigger response forced me to respond in anger to my feelings of worthlessness. I thought Teri would love the outfit and I could tell she didn't (or at least that was my *perception*). Once again, my subconscious replayed an event from my childhood and the thought that I made the wrong decision in buying the outfit for Teri made me feel worthless again. Even though I had excitement and love in my heart as I presented the gift to my wife, it immediately shifted to non-verbal anger when those worthless feelings reached my brain.

And here's the kicker, *maybe* I was wrong about my initial perception that she didn't like the outfit. Maybe it was a color she hadn't worn before and wasn't sure how it looked on her. Maybe she warmed up to the outfit once she saw how she looked in it and after a while, really loved it.

Without that trigger, the whole situation would have played out differently.

It is important to note that triggers are not formed within us only as a child. In the case of abuse that is normally the case but triggers can form based on any traumatic experience in our lives, no matter what age we are.

As I write this book, the tragedy in Newtown, Connecticut just occurred a few weeks ago. This involved many young children being slaughtered by a crazed gunman while they were in school. Whatever sights, sounds, smells, and feelings those first responders experienced as they arrived on scene and witnessed the horror before them, embedded within their subconscious—perhaps forming a trigger response within their mind.

Say for instance, there was a faint smell of pizza in the air as they entered the school because the cafeteria was preparing pizza for the upcoming lunch. The first responders might not have consciously been aware of the pizza smell but their subconscious recorded it. Years later the smell of pizza makes those same first responders relive the exact feelings and physical responses they experienced on that horrific day in December 2012.

They may not have a clue why they flashed back to that day in the school; they don't realize they are having a trigger response to the smell of pizza. But their subconscious knows, and it will continue to fire the "pizza smell" trigger until the first responder seeks help in finding out what the problem is.

Handling Triggers

Triggers are very difficult to break because they happen so quickly. Our brain instantly triggers a response from our subconscious memory banks and we react many times before we can stop and think.

Five years after breaking free from my emotionally abusive behavior, I am still dealing with several triggers within me. Sometimes I instantly react without thinking and sometimes I'm lucky enough to sense my anger building (my *awareness of do*) and am able to defuse my response or exit the situation peacefully.

The key to handling triggers is to take an immediate timeout when the trigger fires. The timeout serves to break the pattern or conditioned response wired into our brain. Remember I said earlier that our brain is wired to circuits that in the past caused our destructive behavior? The timeout begins to short-circuit that circuit which in turn causes the old pattern of destructive behavior to fail.

With some triggers, we are successful in taking a timeout and breaking the pattern immediately - WAHOO! Yet sometimes, we will have to try many times before we are able to break our seemingly instant response. Sometimes it seems the trigger and response occurs before we know what happened. Our partner can assist us and let us know if they perceive we have had a trigger response to something said or done. Our awareness can also help in this area, but it may take effort to even realize we are triggering and take a positive action BEFORE we react negatively to the trigger.

It is important to not get discouraged during our failures and stay positive and focused on the end goal. Remember, every failure brings us one-step closer to success! We did not become abusive overnight and we won't escape our abusive behaviors overnight either. I was abusive for many years so how many years am I willing to give myself to recover?

Through hard work and determination, I have short-circuited many of my old, destructive circuits in my brain, but I am constantly finding ones that remain.

Okay, so we have triggered and have successfully broken our old pattern of behavior (our destructive response) and taken the timeout, now what? I will use the previous lawnmower purchase for an example.

After Teri told me she thought I was being foolish about buying a new lawnmower, and I was able to break my trigger response, I would tell her what I felt when I heard her say I was being foolish. It may take me a few moments to process and get in touch with those feelings, but eventually I would tell her I felt she was saying I made a dumb decision and it made me feel worthless and inadequate.

Of course, this was not her intent when she said she thought I was being foolish, so we would calmly talk about our feelings for a few moments. At this point, I have de-escalated my emotions of anger and childlike behaviors, and am ready to behave as an adult towards Teri and the discussion.

The result of our heated moment is completely different at this point. Trust is being built into the relationship as I show my wife I am making progress on handling my own triggers during the heat of the battle. Intimacy is built between us because I am now able to handle my emotions as an adult instead of a child.

We are building the emotional bond between us, and emotional bonding is exactly what women need in their relationships since women are 90% emotional and 10% sexual (surprise – men are just the opposite). Our marriage is being strengthened instead of being broken down!

This is exciting because what we've just done is called conflict resolution; we figured out a way to arrive at a win-win solution!

This is what a relationship and a marriage is all about my friends. Get a hold of what I presented in these last several sections of the book and your marriage can be much more than you ever thought possible!

In addition, these principles, passed down to our children and our children's children will *forever* break generational relationship dysfunction and destruction.

It WILL take a lot of hard work and it will take a lot of time. There WILL be times when it is easier to simply give up, but whoever said that having something worthwhile and lasting is supposed to be easy?

There is hope! Hang in there!

Chapter 16
Seven Warning Signs Of an Abusive Relationship

The difference between coarse and refined abuse is the difference between being bruised by a club and wounded by a poisoned arrow.
__Johnson

My abusive marriage to Teri took on several forms. There was never any physical abuse and I'm not sure it would be classified as verbal abuse either. My abuse was of the devastatingly emotional kind.

All throughout our marriage, I attempted to convince Teri that my abusive behaviors were just a quark of my personality and she needed to get used to them and make the necessary adjustments to "love me in spite of" and "accept me for who I was."

After so many years, I'm sure I had Teri convinced that it was her fault things weren't better in our marriage, or "if only" she'd try harder to be better or to please me more, everything would be alright.

Baloney!

- If you are being abused, it's important to realize that it's **NOT YOUR FAULT**

- There is **NEVER,** justification for abusing someone else No matter the form - physically, sexually, emotionally, or verbally

- The one abusing needs to seek help and their behaviors are **NEVER** justified or 'enabled'

Here are seven warning signs that you are in an abusive relationship:

Helpless

Helplessness often results when one partner assumes full control over the relationship and attacks the other partner's competence. One person makes all the decision. That person does not hesitate to ridicule or criticize the other in public and in private. Words used like 'stupid,' 'ignorant,' or 'incompetent' are common.

Anxiety

The abusing partner offers no reassurance, stability, or commitment. It is impossible to predict either the behavior or the feelings of the abusing partner or of the relationship. It may be characterized by the "off-again, on-again" pattern or by the abusing partner being frequently unavailable. Actions that produce pleasure one day may provoke verbal or even physical abuse the next.

Hostility

Hostility typically takes the form of aggression, anger, rage and irritability. The abused person responds in kind to the partner's behavior, either openly or privately. The open hostility would be characterized by a raised voice, hurtful or angry words, or accusations against the partner. Private hostility includes such things as hidden resentment, plotted revenge, and private negative fantasies. The hostility may also be internalized as guilt or anger.

Frustration

Frustration results when the abusing partner fails to satisfy needs for affection, intimacy, attention, acceptance, approval, reassurance, praise, or any other emotional need. No matter how hard the partner tries to please the other, it never is enough. They will praise others but never mention your own achievements. They "work the room" but leave you standing alone in the corner.

Cynicism

Any action, which constitutes a betrayal or abuse of trust, is likely to result in cynicism. Obviously having an affair with another person fits into this category. Additionally, patterns of borrowing money which is never repaid, making promises which are seldom kept, or sharing information given in confidence will likely produce cynicism.

Loss of Self-Esteem

This sign includes feelings of diminished self-worth, inadequacy, negative self-image, reduced self-confidence, and deterioration of self-respect, with associated depression. Choosing to remain in a relationship in which a person feels devalued inevitably leads to increased loss of self-esteem.

Loss of self-esteem happens through a cycle of faulty logic: First, you recognize that you are in a relationship in which you feel unloved, unworthy, and mistreated. That you would choose such a relationship causes you to doubt your judgment. Your try to "fix" it by changing yourself or your partner, but when that does not work you conclude that you not only have poor judgment, you also are inept at relationship skills.

Thus, you reason "people get what they deserve," and since you are being treated badly, you must deserve it. Obviously, then, the only thing for you to do is to accept the treatment since you "don't deserve" nor could ever hope for a better relationship.

Hopelessness

Hopelessness usually results after numerous vain attempts to communicate the need for a change, with the partner ignoring all approaches. A person who recognizes a lack of responsiveness is their partner can be warned from the beginning that the relationship is developing in an unhealthy manner and there is likely trouble ahead.

You do have options if you're in an abusive relationship but recognizing you're in one is the first step.

tips, traits, n 'tudes

Chapter 17
Tips, Traits, n 'tudes

Action may not always bring happiness; but there is no happiness without action. __Disraeli

Is it possible to be free of abusive behavior for good? If you have read the book to this point, you know what I have been saying all along - it is not easy... but it is doable. Have hope!

Before digging in to some tips that may help along the way, I must remind you once again, I am not a professional in psychology nor any type of counselor.

I AM NOT GIVING MEDICAL ADVICE HERE.

I only have *my* experiences of 30-years as an abuser and the past five years in recovery from that abuse to share; along with approximately 150 hours in classroom training, as well as a several people that I have been fortunate enough to meet that have also had their lives impacted by abuse. Bottom line—I am hardly an expert.

However, I do know what worked for me and I believe some of the things I will discuss will work for you too.

I cannot stress enough to seek professional help when trying to deal with any aspect of emotional abuse. I could write 500 pages about breaking free from emotional abuse, but I believe with all my heart that you *must* have someone you trust walk beside you as you begin your journey to freedom, and that person needs to have *specific* training in dealing with abusive behavior and all its nuances.

DO NOT TRY TO GO THIS ALONE. It will not work—period.

As I've said all along, my intentions of this book are to share my experience and in doing so, *hopefully* raise an awareness level in someone like yourself, so you can *begin* to face the truth in your own life, ask for help, and *begin* your journey of healing from this devastating illness.

Nothing would make me happier than receiving an email knowing that this book was successful in helping someone do just that—begin!

DO NOT think following my suggestions alone will break you out of a pattern of abusive behavior. It might for a short time but I am confident you are not looking for a *short term* answer are you? No. Not when you can have an everlasting change within you and be free FOREVER of the chains that held you captive for so long.

For your sake and the sake of those you love, GET PROFESSIONAL HELP!

Enough said...

During the past five years, I have had an opportunity to speak with several people in the process of breaking free from their own abusive behaviors. As we each talked about our journey, I began to notice a common thread in us all; common traits that we all possessed.

When I compared our common set of traits with men who had not seemed to have their breakthrough yet and start *their* journey away from abuse, I noticed they appeared to be missing one or more of these traits.

So that led me to believe that there has to be a common thread, a glue if you will, that sticks all the 'things' together that we must unlearn, learn, and relearn in order to be free from abuse.

We have SO much brokenness in us when we first start our journey to freedom. We have to unlearn so many things that we thought were true, while at the same time inserting new thoughts and truths (THE truth). We have to stop old patterns of behavior that are destructive and force knew healthy patterns in their place.

Moreover, we have to slowly begin to trust ourselves again... all the while KNOWING that those around us, whom we love, do NOT trust us, not initially at least. Many times, we have to form a new self-confidence out of nothing but the ashes of our former self.

In my own experience, when I finally woke up to the truth, it seemed just about *everything* I used to think was real, was fake; everything I thought was fact was fiction. I was dealing with dozens of emotions... all at the same time.

I was dealing with all the hundreds of times my behaviors negatively affected those that I love. I was dealing with an extreme amount of grieve, guilt, and shame... all at the same time. I had to stand and look in the mirror, and be willing to accept every reflection that came back at me, regardless of how grotesque they appeared!

Moreover, I was dealing with so many new insecurities about the *new me* because I didn't know if my new behaviors were still controlling, manipulative, and abusive or not. I didn't trust myself, and I was constantly second guessing myself. I was scared and I was ticked that I allowed myself to fall into this trap!

Fortunately for me, I had the Lord standing right with me the whole time, guiding me. However, it was still up to me to take each slow, painful step out of my own self-imposed torment.

So what are the traits I discovered?

- Awareness
- Willingness to be taught new things

- Stick-to-itiveness attitude

- Vision

Having awareness is the same thing as standing and taking a hard look into that mirror. It starts with becoming aware of *who* we were as an abuser. It continues with having a conscious awareness of the things we do and say on a daily basis. We must have an awareness to inform us if we have hurt, controlled or manipulated in any way. Alternatively, we must have an awareness when we are about to be caught in a situation where we might be tempted to get angry, or allow our buttons to be pushed.

We have to be completely open-minded and *willing to learn new things* and to change our mind based on new information we receive. We have to be willing to accept criticism and the faults that lie within us without slipping back into our old ways of defensiveness or focusing on the faults of those around us instead of our own.

We have to have an *attitude* that flat says we're going to do whatever it takes to get healthy. If we fail at something fifty times, we'll try it fifty-one. We will never give up until we reach our breakthrough. It's the least we can do for ourselves, our higher power, and the ones we love.

Finally, we have to have a *vision* – a goal. We have to be able to see some form of the end even before we start. We will never hit a target that we cannot see. We have to believe that goal is obtainable no matter what obstacles come our way. I will talk more about this in a bit.

Breaking free from the chains that bound us and held us prisoner for many, many years, perhaps for as long as we can remember, is never easy – just worth it.

Give Yourself a Break

Breaking free from abuse will be an ongoing process for us. We will have many times when we mess up, slip back to our old ways, and generally feel like we might NEVER learn to behave differently and break free from our destructive ways!

WE have to learn to give ourselves a break along the way. Cut ourselves some slack. We must realize we did not become abusive overnight and we will not break free from it overnight either.

I slipped up plenty of times the first year it seemed, and still do occasionally even after five years. I realized over time even my screw ups were a 'victory' because I was making progress—I was *aware* I messed up. This realization was a major step in the right direction because in the past I had no clue how destructive my behavior was.

I did not have a clue that I walked around with such unrealistic expectations about everyone around me. No clue I was angry so many days of my life and powerless to that anger. I had no clue to the effects that anger was having on Teri and the kids. No clue the reactions to my world were based on a twelve-year-old child rather than an adult.

Therefore, in those times when I would mess up and say or do the wrong thing, I had to realize just *knowing* I did the wrong thing was huge. The knowing (awareness) gave me options. It allowed me to strive to do better the next time. I could face my shortcomings and mistakes as an adult rather than a child.

So go easy on yourself in all this. It *will* take time to learn to shift focus away from others and onto yourself. It *will* take time to develop new patterns of thought and behavior in your mind. You are literally rewiring the circuitry in your brain and that my friend is a very tedious, time consuming and sometimes - maddening process.

This is a war, which will be won one small battle at a time. Some battles you will lose, some you will win. Over time, you will reflect over the past and be able to measure real progress.

For those of you who are currently being abused and have committed to helping your mate break free from their abusive behavior, it is important to allow plenty of room while your mate readjusts to new ways of dealing with daily life. This will be difficult for you as well.

Each time your mate slips back to their "old ways" of doing things, it will reinforce in your mind *they will never change*. It is important to measure change in months rather than days or weeks. I hope that you will notice some changes very quickly as your partner becomes aware of their abusive behavior. That will serve to give you a bit of confidence that change can occur.

I applaud your willingness to hang in there through difficult times. You have many emotional wounds and scars to heal within yourself and this will be a difficult process for you, no doubt.

Realizing this is a journey of a million steps filled with potholes and detours along the way will help to take some of the pressure of us. Each misstep is a chance to learn. Every rainy day will eventually see the sun break through. Stay focused on your goals during those times and you will find a way to achieve them!

Goals

We must have a goal and be able to maintain a vision of that goal throughout our journey. We cannot hit a target that we do not see. I'm not necessarily talking about sitting down and writing a long list of goals that we would like to achieve during this process (though that's an option), but I do believe we need to have a clear vision in our mind of what we plan to achieve.

There is something called the pain pleasure principle which says we will be motivated by either pain or by pleasure. People will usually do more to avoid pain than they will to seek pleasure even though pleasure, ultimately, is what they are after. Many times we will not do what we know needs to be done, and we want done, until the pain of *not* doing it becomes so great that we are motivated to start.

For the abuser, pain is often our initial motivator to change. We must reach bottom and wallow in the filth for a while before the pain of staying there, and possibly losing everything we have and want, *forces* us to change. However, once the changes begin, it is important to use goals and vision to motivate us in a positive way rather than using pain as a negative motivator to steer us away from our negative behaviors.

A clear, positive vision of what we see for the future becomes that pleasure and keeps us motivated through the tough times.

For me, I had a burning desire to become mentally healthy – which meant no control, manipulation, or abuse of any kind – and to see my marriage restored and become vibrant. I had a deep desire to reform healthy relationships with my children and to become a positive role model, displaying qualities that they would like to see in a man who may eventually become their husband.

Though my desire for my marriage did not pan out, I did achieve my goal to become healthy and break free from control, manipulation, and abuse. I am still working on my third goal of forming healthy relationships with my children. The vision I keep in my head of what a *healthy relationship* looks like is what keeps me going through a continuing up and down process five years after it began.

Honesty & Transparency

We must commit to being completely honest and transparent with others and our self as we progress down the path to our healing. We must be what I call, *being open*. As we open ourselves to others, we must allow them to be honest with us. It will take time and effort to get comfortable doing this, but as we experience the freedom and trust it brings; we will slowly begin to embrace it.

Being honest means we are completely truthful in three areas:

- Our past behavior and the hurts and pains they caused—to our self and to others

- Our current successes, failures, behaviors, and feelings as we move along on our journey to wholeness and health

- The painful memories and feelings from our childhood that we have spent a lifetime keeping hidden and stuffed into deep, dark recesses of our mind

Being transparent means, we are willing to peel back the layers of the onion and expose these three areas to examination. This means examination by our self and by others. It's scary as heck to be totally honest and transparent, and allow ourselves to be at the mercy of others. We are giving them permission to accept or reject us. We are allowing ourselves to be vulnerable.

This is a new situation for us; we have always protected our true self—our real pains. We have more than likely never shared *completely*, with anyone, our childhood memories and traumas— perhaps we've done such a good job of stuffing and hiding them that we haven't discovered many of them for our self yet.

However, the payoff to our well-being is too great to ignore. We must press through the fear and uncertainty to gain our freedom... and victory!

Honesty & Transparency with Oneself

It is not easy to look within our self and admit the truth of our abuse and all the damage our abuse caused, but it is the first step in the recovery process. Once we are willing to be completely honest, there is an internal pressure that seems to release and we can begin to detach our self from the old behavior and reattach to the real person we are—the new person that we will be.

I'm sure there's some psychological term for this detachment, but I'll attempt to define it through my own experience of what happened during my journey.

When I discovered I was a 30-year abuser, it took several weeks for me to come to grips with that reality. I knew it was true and the overwhelming grief of the pain I caused, along with realizing I was a mess and a failure for most of my life, took a while to settle within me.

Once that settling occurred, I began to look at my abusive behaviors as something other than who I was in the present. I was still a mess, yes, but I was a mess who no longer had the desire to control, manipulate, or abuse. The inner child I was protecting all those years was exposed, and I could face my situation, those I hurt, and life in general, as an adult. I didn't quite know *how* to face the future, but I knew I would with a different mind, attitude, and behavior.

It was much easier for me to be completely open about my abuse and the pain it caused (I caused) because I was no longer attached to it – it didn't define who I was in the present. I still owned all of the past behaviors and the pain they inflicted of course, but owning them did not diminish who I was now.

I found the more open I was about my past behavior, those behaviors no longer held their power over me. My self-worth was no longer tied to those abusive behaviors because they didn't define me, as a person any longer. I could be honest and transparent about the past because the past did not equal my future.

This detachment also allowed me to discover the truth about what happened to me as a child. With the help of others, over a period of several months, I was able to look into my past, discover the origins of my abuse, and release those responsible and the pain they caused me.

I believe my willingness to lay myself bare to people I trusted was instrumental in making those discoveries so quickly.

We must be willing to own our past behavior and actions when we talk to our mate, children and others we hurt, never forgetting the pain and damage we inflicted upon them nor the scars that may remain for a good number of years.

It is critical to remember that we may have detached from our old behavior and *put them in the past*, but it will more than likely take our family quite a while before they are able to do the same. We must have empathy for them as they take time to heal from *their* wounds and perhaps learn to trust us for the very first time.

As we share our current thoughts, feelings, behaviors, and struggles with those closest to us, and receive their feedback without becoming defensive, those struggles and our past patterns of behavior begin to lose their power and control over us. We no longer have to be ashamed of them; they are merely obstacles to overcome on our way to achieving our goals.

Trust and intimacy begin to build in our marriage and relationships as we talk openly about the reality of who we were and who we are trying to become, while giving our mate permission to talk openly about their feelings and experiences as they too begin to heal.

This new level of openness will be counter-intuitive to the way things were handled in the past, so there will be many starts, stops, and frustrations along the way, as we get comfortable with new ways of communicating feelings. There will be times when old behaviors come crashing through. Those times will be frustrating for us as we try to figure out what areas of our past need to be healed.

For our mates whom we abused, those times may reinforce their fear that we are slipping back to our old self and will never be able to change. Those feelings of fear may take years to subside.

I have talked to women who many years after their husbands were completely free of control, manipulation, and abuse; have been fearful that he was slipping back to a form of his old self whenever they detected an old pattern of behavior in him. The behavior itself was not abusive; it merely triggered (there's those triggers again) a fear in their mind that the behavior was their abusive mate's persona coming out. It took them many years to completely trust again.

Honesty and transparency have the power to unlock areas of your relationship and marriage that have been closed off for quite some time—more than likely, forever. This is an area that will take each of you many months and perhaps years to get a comfort level in. Individual counseling from professionals with experience in helping couples break free from abuse is important.

As I've said before, it will be difficult but it will be oh so worth it. You will experience new levels of trust and intimacy that have never been present before and you will probably be the envy of your friends and neighbors.

Go for it!

Journaling

Let's be honest, if we have not kept a journal in the past, disciplining our self to do so will be a royal pain! To this day I will go through periods when I will journal regularly and periods when I will not journal at all. So be it. That is just the way I am and I quit pressuring myself a few years ago.

HOWEVER...

I have done a good enough job keeping a written log of my thoughts (that is a journal, eh?) to be able to read and see tangible proof of my progress (and struggles) over the years. And that is the whole point of keeping a journal when trying to break free from abuse —knowing we are making progress.

In the last three sections I talked about giving yourself a break, goals, and learning to be more transparent. How are we going to measure our progress in those areas? We will have dozens of little successes and failures along the way as the overall trend continues to a more positive behavior.

If we do not have some method of tracking that trend, over a period of months, we will not know whether we are making real progress, and more importantly, keeping track of those small hits and misses along the way. Being able to look back over a written record of our journey is very helpful and will help remind us of things long forgotten.

I cannot stress enough to always keep a notebook or a few sheets of paper folded and kept in a pocket or even a few index cards (and pen!) carried with us at all times. There will be many times when we will act or react a certain way and it's important we keep a log of our thoughts, memories and feelings *at the time they occur* and not try and remember those feelings later when we get back home or later on that evening.

Our triggers, anger and Arrested Development all stem from points of time in our past. As I've talked about all throughout this book, remembering those points in time are *critical* to releasing them and breaking free from their grip and power they have over us.

We need to keep something near when go to bed too. It's amazing how many things will come into our mind while we're asleep or while we are dreaming. It's always best if we can wake up and make a few notes as soon as possible rather than thinking we will remember the thought or dream in the morning.

I've had dreams or thoughts in the middle of the night that I *knew* I'd remember when I awoke in the morning, only to find myself not having a clue what it was I was supposed to remember. Not a clue! I now sleep with a small dictation device on the bed beside me so I can record those thoughts without having to sit up and turn on a light.

Sometimes my recorded thoughts don't make a lot of sense when I listen to them but they have jogged something in my memory later on in the day or even a few days later!

Journaling and keeping track of our thoughts and whatever else comes to your mind as you journey down our recovery pathway is an excellent way to record our progress. I enjoy looking back over my old journals from time to time and read about my thoughts and mindsets of the past.

Many times, I will look back to the first time I discovered a new truth that helped me to break further and further away from who I was. In those times, I am so thankful that though I have got a long way to go, I am certainly not where I used to be!

Chapter 18
Timeouts

A wise man reflects before he speaks. –A fool speaks, and then reflects on what he has uttered. ___De Lille

Timeouts are not just for kids!

Timeouts are useful to break many of the patterns of behavior that seem to be on autopilot in our mind. We act or react, many times, *without thinking* it seems. The timeout concept is the same many of us have used on our children—stop the current pattern of behavior, place them in a quiet place to cool down, and give them time to reflect.

There are two different timeouts I'll discuss; one is self-imposed, used to stop a conversation with someone from potentially getting worse, and the other is useful between couples because it involves a contract—a Timeout Contract.

Both timeouts follow the same basic format that I'll discuss below—cool down, reflect and reconvene. The Timeout Contract for couples specifies a mutual signal to use to signal a timeout is needed, along with other dos and don'ts during the actual timeout.

The Timeout

Whenever we feel our self starting to ramp up the anger, or starting to move to more abusive behavior such as belittling, dragging up the past, or becoming defensive, we need to break the pattern of behavior and take a timeout to reflect on our feelings, thoughts, and actions.

In order to identify a need for a timeout, we must rely on our *awareness of do* to alert us to a potentially dangerous scenario approaching.

Breaking our pattern, *during the heat of the moment*, is the challenging part. In the midst of buttons being pushed, nerves becoming frayed, anger being awakened, and topped off with a surge of adrenaline that comes with these emotions, it is very difficult to think clearly and put the brakes on our behavior *before* it happens.

Many times, we will blow right past our awareness of what is happening, and continue elevating our words and behavior. If we don't learn to short-circuit the destructive patterns, a meltdown more than likely ensues.

How do we short-circuit those destructive patterns? I believe when we become aware of our abuse, an internal alarm is planted within us, what I referred to as our *awareness of do* in a previous chapter. This alarm goes off to warn us, but many times the noise of our anger drowns out the sound of the alarm. We must learn to listen for this alarm, trust it, heed its warning, and STOP OUR BEHAVIOR!

I know in talking with others who are successfully overcoming their abuse, the alarm is within each of us. We must choose whether we are going to stick with it and learn to alter our behavior by responding to the alarm or not. I stated earlier that our awareness only serves one purpose; it offers us a chance to make a choice - change or don't change, it's up to us to decide.

Cool Down

Okay, after a few tries, we have broken our pattern of behavior, removed our self from the situation, and taken the timeout, now it's time to cool down and reflect. Most times it is best to do something - go for a walk, take a drive, do chores, etc., to get our focus off the other person and onto *our* feelings and behaviors.

We need to be honest with our self as we do a self-evaluation. This is where honesty and transparency comes in to play. It will be difficult at first because it's human nature to blame outside events or other people for our behavior. We must constantly remind our self that we are responsible for our own actions, regardless of the other person's actions.

The cool down period is a time to reflect and figure out a way to constructively continue the discussion without escalating our emotions. Even if it was the other person's behavior that caused us to get angry, there are still things we can do to figure out why *their* behavior affected *us* so much. If it was our own behavior that got out of line, we need to reflect and figure out what feelings of ours caused it.

There are two realities we must look at here—our *perceived* reality and the *real* reality. Our perceived reality is what we thought or how we felt based on the other person's behavior or words towards us. In my example of the lawnmower earlier, when Teri said I was being foolish for considering buying a new mower, I *perceived* she was scolding me about my "dumb decision," and that she felt I was worthless and inadequate.

Of course, it wasn't Teri's intent to convey those thoughts to me at all, but that is what I perceived she was telling me, based on a subconscious trigger of mine from my childhood.

The *real* reality was that my feelings of being worthless and inadequate stemmed from the way my father treated me when I was a child. My current feelings had nothing to do with Teri, other than her statement to me triggered an automated, subconscious response based on a childhood event.

While in our timeout, we need to ask our self if we triggered as the result of a feeling from an earlier time in our lives of perhaps embarrassment, rejection, insecurity, or anger. If so, we should be able to go to the other person and explain what our *perceived* feelings were based on what they said to us and what the underlying *real* feelings were that caused us to have those perceived feelings.

That might be all that is necessary to get the conversation back on track and precede to a successful conclusion. However, at some point, we need to process those feelings a little more in order to release the control they have over us.

When I first started using timeouts, I wrote down some basic questions on a card that I would grab before I went for a walk to cool down. Due to my brokenness, it was sometimes very difficult to get my mind off the other person's behavior and having a few questions to get me refocused helped. Things we may ask our self are:

- At what point did we begin to lose it?

  - Something the other person said?

  - The way they said it?

  - Was it a body response or a certain look?

  - Maybe it was seeing their anger that triggered us.

- What were we feeling to cause our anger or defensiveness?
  - Hurt?
  - Embarrassment?
  - Inadequacy?
  - Rejection?

- Insecurity?

The purpose of the cool down is to get in touch with our *real* feelings that forced off off-track during the discussion, or they will continue to derail us going forward. We may feel it's as if a wall is around those real feelings, protecting them, but we must break through our own protective mechanisms that are sealing those feelings off from us in order to get at the root of our anger or defensiveness.

As an abuser, we have gotten quite good at masking our real feelings and responding in anger based on our perceived feelings.

Do not minimize the time you need in order to take a hard, realistic look into your own feelings here and get to the root of your real feelings. It is not fun initially but it is critical to a healthy recovery.

We *may* be tempted to short change our self, get to the point where we are no longer angry with the other person and think *that is good enough,* and not take the time to get to those darn feelings, but we must!

Have we cooled down enough to resume the conversation? A good question to ask our self is does the thought of seeing or talking to the other person make us think of what they said or did *to us* earlier? Does it make us angry or *miffed* at all? If so, we need more time to process our feelings and emotions. We need more time in timeout. Don't be shy about taking whatever time is needed at this point.

What to do after the Timeout

There are three choices we have after our timeout:

- Drop it
- Put the discussion on hold
- Discuss it

We need to come to a decision and choose one of the three choices and *follow through*. This is not a time to fool our self and believe we have cooled down and decide to drop or put the discussion on hold, when in truth, we still harbor anger, bitterness or resentment.

We cannot allow our self to fall back into the same patterns and beliefs we had while being abusive. Being *completely* honest and transparent with our self at this point is critical!

Drop it

If we've decided to drop the issue because we realized the issue is no longer a concern for us, great, then drop it and move on—but *only* if it's still not an issue for the other person as well.

If there are unresolved issues the other person is dealing with, then we cannot simply decide to drop the matter and leave the other person hanging. We need to allow them to have their say and it's important we approach them and ask to either put the issue on hold for a while or, discuss the issue if they are ready.

If we decide to drop the issue but after a short period of time find our self replaying the issue in our mind or think of the other person's transgressions towards us, no matter how brief the thoughts, than it's a *clear sign* we haven't really dropped the issue (been there done that!). We are still harboring ill feelings, blame, or bitterness towards the other person and we MUST readdress what our *real* feelings are again.

If we do not readdress the issue, bitterness, no matter how well hidden within, *will* turn to resentment and *will* manifest its ugly head at some point in the future. This is the very thing that has been going on inside us for a very long time—stuffing our true feelings because we don't know how to process them.

I cannot stress how important it is to not give up on this; to press through your *perceived* feelings to get in touch with your inner, real feelings—no matter how hard or no matter where those feelings lead you.

If we're a guy, this is NOT easy for us to do—all this "feelings stuff!" We have been told probably our whole life to stuff our feelings and "be a man." But I can assure you, it takes a REAL man to be in touch with his feelings.

I am SO thankful that I am finally able to get in touch with mine. I don't have to be afraid of them anymore! Plus, the ladies love it when we are comfortable enough in our manliness to display a little 'feeling' every once in a while. Learn to connect emotionally with that wife of yours and watch her respond in ways you've never seen before—let the sparks ignite (if you know what I mean).

But, the bottom line is, all of this is crucial to getting all that we want—a healthy mind, healthy relationships and inner peace.

Okay, sorry, back on topic...

Put the Discussion on Hold

If we have decided to put the decision on hold, then make sure to set a period when the issue will be readdressed with the other person—and stick to it! Failure to come up with an agreement of *a couple days,* or whenever, will once again open the doors to thinking the issue will go away on its own while in truth, the issue remains hidden within us.

If we simply tell the other person "We'll talk about it later" and 'later' never comes, that is not good enough my friend. Once again, *old patterns of behavior* are surfacing. The bottom line – we must set a realistic period with the other person to revisit the discussion and then stick to our agreement to get back together.

Discuss It

A great way to reopen a discussion is with a heartfelt apology. There is always something we can be sorry about that happened prior to the timeout being called. It is best not to try to give justifications for our actions or words, just say we were wrong, apologize, and ask for forgiveness.

After apologizing, it's important to listen, and then wait for our chance to listen some more to the other person as they explain their feelings and emotions so you have a good understanding of where they are coming from in the issue.

You may hear their perceived feelings instead of their real feelings regarding the discussion.

You may not agree with what they are saying to you, but you at least allowed them a chance to restate their feelings. It is important that we do not allow ourselves to become defensive when we hear the other person's feelings directed at us. We must not interrupt.

To this day, I have trouble allowing the other person to speak fully. I find myself interrupting all too often. Some internal habits are very hard to break but it is only through the repetition of failing, recognizing, and trying again that the rewiring of our brains will be accomplished.

It is at times a very frustrating process, one of which you will sometimes think you'll *never* learn what is necessary but I can assure you, as someone who was the most broken of the broken, it *can* and will happen IF you do one thing – stay with it.

Now we have a chance to express our feelings. It's okay to be direct, something like "I feel hurt and angry when it seems like you are talking down to me. I think you don't care how I feel and I want to lash back at you in anger." It's weird but if we are willing to say something like this to our wife, more than likely, they will feel closer to us!

We being open and vulnerable enough to share our feelings with them is HUGE in their mind and something they are not used to seeing. Good job! We are showing we know how to process our feelings without using anger to protect them.

Even though I may write as if this is an easy process, it is NOT. I know by experience. I went through many times of frustration, being upset and simply not wanting to do all or any of this. It was easier just to ignore all this *feelings stuff* and move on. I know, this is *not* an easy process to learn. However, there is no other way my friend. So I say, be frustrated, be upset that you think you'll never *get it*, that you are making zero progress... but stay with it.

This is a good time to journal our thoughts and emotions, track our fears, frustrations, anger, whatever. We are learning.

Every time we simply recognize an old, destructive pattern is a win! How many times in the past did we exhibit those exact same destructive patterns yet have NO CLUE we were doing anything wrong or worse yet, thought *we* were right!?

Lastly, and most importantly, if at *any time* during the discussion you feel that inner rage starting to build yet again—S T O P! Take another timeout. You might be able to regroup quickly and continue the discussion or you might need an extended timeout (whatever you need take it).

Having to take multiple timeouts to get through a single discussion is not unexpected, especially since your mate may be repeating some of their old patterns and allowing their buttons to be pushed without realizing it.

You might need to be the one to take the lead in calling for some additional time. If at any time you recognize that you may be losing control to those self-destructive behaviors, call the timeout.

Don't use the other person's behavior as an excuse for your negative feelings, emotions or behavior. This may very well be the natural path you want to take but that is the very reason not to. Own your own feelings and emotions.

You WILL Get it

Do not worry my friend, you will only have to repeat this process a hundred times or so before it becomes second nature for you.

I am with you every step of the way.

It WILL get easier and, the feelings of freedom you begin to experience with be like nothing else. Confidence will begin to eek its way into your soul and you will perhaps begin to see a small, very small light at the end of the tunnel.

For the recovering abuser, timeouts are a great tool to carry with us at all times.

Chapter 19
Using a Timeout Contract

Let us watch well our beginnings, and results will manage themselves.
__Alex Clark

Teri and I came across using a Timeout Contract some years ago and found it to be an effective tool even though I was still in my abusive state. We found a way to stop an argument from quickly getting out of control or perhaps a discussion from turning into an argument.

We also discovered once we both took some time to cool down and reflect before continuing the discussion, many of the things that we were getting *hot-n-bothered* about during the discussion just weren't that big of a deal.

The contract is shown at the end of this chapter. I will go over the different sections here (except for the obvious - Name, etc.).

The cues that indicate I'm getting angry are:

Do a self-evaluation and determine what are some of the changes you notice in your voice, inflection, or body that indicate your anger is starting to rise. For instance, I would list 1) louder tone of voice, 2) interrupt other person, 3) a rage boils up within me, 4) exaggerated movements - pointing, arms flailing, eyes get bigger, and 5) feel flush in my face.

My mate's triggers I need to avoid are:

What do you say or do that you *know* gets your mate worked up? If you are inclined to say "Nothing," asks your mate—they will be able to list one, or six. List the ones you know of and ask your mate if there are one or two perhaps you do/say that you weren't aware of. For me I would list 1) disrespectful and not listening, 2) belittling or patronizing words, 3) mimicking her facial expressions, 4) cursing, and 5) walking away.

These will help you avoid saying or doing things that intentionally set your mate off. Sometimes when we are hurt, we do hurtful things. If during a discussion/argument either of you use any of the triggers listed, call for a timeout!

Neutral signal we will use to signal a time out is:

Select some type of verbal or non-verbal signal that will be used to indicate a timeout is needed. This could be a word or phrase - "We need a timeout" or some hand signal - a "T" indicating "timeout." If at ANY time this signal is given by either person, the discussion needs to end, right then, and each of you go your separate ways.

No taking the time to try to explain what you just said prior to the signal being given or saying something like "Okay, time out, but can I just finish what I was trying to say?" There needs to be NO conversation directly related to the discussion that led to a timeout signal being given. This will be difficult to put into practice initially but is critical if you're serious about using a Timeout Contract effectively.

We will each go to an isolated location, away from our mate when either of us gives the signal.

Once a timeout is called for, it is time to go to your own private areas away from each other in order to cool down and begin to process the conversation and your feelings. Take a walk, do some gardening, listen to some soothing music; there is no need to lock yourself in a room during this time, unless that is the best way you process things.

An example of something that might not work too well would be the husband going to the family room and the wife must go to the kitchen (next to the family room) to fix dinner for the kids. Split up! Normally the mere presence of the mate can be a mental distraction when trying to cool down and self-evaluate your own part of the discussion getting out of hand. Split up and get by yourself for the agreed upon time.

No "final word," name-calling or slamming doors once the timeout signal is given

This goes along with what I mentioned above pertaining to the neutral signal to use for a timeout. These are just some examples of things that might be done once the time out signal is given by one or both parties to try and get that last "jab" in or let the other person know just how hurt you are or just how mad they made you, or, get the final word in before splitting up. Do not do it.

Feel free to use your own experiences to adjust this contract item.

I will abide by my partner's signal and immediately leave the area

This is self-explanatory. No hanging around. Your partner needs a time out - they recognize their own anger beginning to rise or they recognize it in you. Regardless, respect their decision, shut down the conversation and go cool off.

The cool down period shall be for a minimum of:

Set a minimum time each of you will take to cool down and process - say thirty or sixty minutes or so. This time should be set to allow you each a comfortable amount of time to do what is needed and reconvene with your mate.

If more time is needed than get back together with your mate after the agreed upon time and state, your desire to have more time and then set a new time limit. Each partner needs to be respectful of the other person's requirement for time to process things.

At the end of the time out, we will:

This is where you will set some agreed up action items to perform when the timeout is over. You can use the three decisions I outlined in the *Timeouts* section —drop it, put the discussion on hold, or discuss it.

Remember, to receive grace is to give grace.

Rules during the timeout are:

I started with a few rules that are vital - no drugs, alcohol, or caffeine. Emotions are already amped up, and stimulants are not going to help and will most likely cause further problems.

Some other things to consider could be "no shopping" if financial issues are already an issue in the relationship or "no driving" if one of you tends to be a little reckless when driving while angry or perhaps "no computer."

One or both of you should have a good idea what rules, if any, to add here based on previous experience but if not, don't sweat it. After a few timeouts, you will have one or more rules to add.

Sign it

Both parties need to sign and date the contract and it is best to keep it somewhere handy for reference if needed. You might be one of the lucky ones who take to the contract quickly and smoothly or, you might be like most of the rest of us and there will be some trial and error initially or, one or both of you will forget all about any *stupid contract* once each other's buttons have been pushed.

As with all learned behavior, learning new things takes time and a commitment. As I said above, even with me still being sick and in an abusive state of mind, Teri and I found this Timeout Contract helpful.

It took a while to get used to it, especially when I am getting angry, Teri would flash the "T" symbol to me, and I had to instantly stop what I was saying. Not easy for a control freak!

Many times seeing those crossed hands would make me angrier because I simply didn't WANT to stop. Nevertheless, I realized the importance of diffusing the situation for a time period and I would comply and go off and stew for quite a while and many times would have to "re-up" the timeout period but, eventually I saw the benefit of using this contract and we got things worked out and it became easier.

If you'd like a copy of the contract on the next page, feel free to email me at austin.f.james@gmail.com with the words "timeout contract" in the subject line, and I'll be glad to send you a .doc file of the contract shown on the next page, or a .pdf if you would prefer.

TIMEOUT CONTRACT

Name:_____	Name:_____
The cues to indicate I'm getting angry are:	*The cues to indicate I'm getting angry are:*
_____	_____
_____	_____
_____	_____
_____	_____
My mate's triggers I need to avoid are:	*My mate's triggers I need to avoid are:*
_____	_____
_____	_____
_____	_____
_____	_____

The neutral signal we will use to signal a timeout is _____.

We will each go to an isolated location, away from our mate, when the signal is given by either of us.

There shall be no "final word/comment", name calling, slamming of doors, etc when timeout signal is given.

I will abide by my partner's signal and immediately leave the area.

The cool down period shall be for a minimum of _____.

At the end of the time out we will _____

_____

Rules during the time out are: <u>no drugs, no alcohol, no caffeine</u>_____

_____

_____

Signed: _____   Signed: _____

Printed:_____   Printed:_____

Date: _____   Date: _____

getting help

Chapter 20
Getting Help
Through Counselling

Good counsel observed, are chains to grace, which, neglected, prove halter to strange, undutiful children. __Fuller

I certainly think counseling has its merits in an abusive relationship, but I think it is going to take some effort to find a counselor who is going to be effective in dealing with both an abuser and the one being abused.

The natural tendency for couples is to look for a marriage counselor because the marriage is where the problem of abuse manifests itself most notably.

It is my opinion that *most* professionals trained in marriage counseling are not trained to deal with emotional abuse and the deep psychological scars that are so interlaced together.

Oversimplifying here, the underlying problem that you and your mate are facing is not one of learning to give and take in the marriage, or learning how to deal with your mate's idiosyncrasies and tendencies that drive you nuts.

Before any of those issues can be addressed, the abuser must learn to deal with the underlying psychological wounds that were inflicted at an early age of their childhood. It is a lot like peeling an onion, one difficult layer at a time. This takes intense individual counseling and is not the forte of most marriage counselors, nor should it be.

Until the abuser gets individual counseling, couples counseling is not going to work—trust me I know.

Teri and I went to five different professional marriage counselors during our twenty-four year marriage, and spent a ton of money. Teri *always* brought up 'anger' as the underlying issue in our relationship, yet not a single counselor mentioned abuse during any of our sessions.

It's not that the counselors were bad counselors; they were not trained in emotional abuse and did not know to probe for the signs of abuse when the anger issue surfaced between us.

Emotional abuse is becoming more and more understood but there is still a long way to go before effective treatment from professionals can be found. I don't mean to dissuade you from looking for a counselor, but be prepared to put some work into finding one.

Note: The marriage counselor that your best friend or coworker recommends, probably is not going to be equipped to deal with something like emotional abuse.

Something as complex as emotional abuse cannot be treated with both parties present in counseling at the same time. You *must* have individual and independent counseling before you can hope to do counseling as a couple. Emotional abuse affects the couple but it is an individual disorder, not a couple one.

The mate caught in their abusive mindset must deal with their own awareness of who they were along with all the feelings of pain, guilt, and shame that go along with it.

They must also deal with the childhood trauma that led to their abuse and release all of the hurt, pain, and feelings associated with that trauma. In a word, they must become healthy as an individual before they can ever hope to help the marriage become healthy.

The one being abused needs to go through an equally hard and painful process in dealing with how and why they allowed themselves to become a victim. I don't mean to be harsh to those of you who have suffered through many years of your mate's abusive behavior. However, there are underlying issues, probably stemming from your childhood as well, that prevented you from realizing what was going on and being able to put a stop to it.

This is not you putting a stop to your abusive mate's behavior, you cannot do that, but putting a stop to you being a victim of their behavior. Make sense?

To find a counselor I would recommend simply calling a around and asking if they have experience in dealing with emotional abuse. If they do, I would find a way early in the question and answer process to ask them a simple question "Do you counsel us as a couple?" If they say "Yes," look elsewhere.

If on the other hand a counselor answers "No," chances are they have experience in dealing with the subject and would warrant additional interviewing to see if you feel they are a good match for you and your situation.

Other things I would want to know are what role they felt a person's childhood plays in emotional abuse. I would be more comfortable dealing with a counselor who felt a person's childhood is critical to the success in treating emotional abuse.

Again, I am not a professional, but I can't imagine there are too many cases where a person's childhood did *not* play a role in the development of their emotionally abuse behavior.

I would want to know how many years they've been dealing with treating emotional abuse and what they felt was the key criteria in determining whether the abusive mate was ready to enter counseling as a couple. Is *awareness* part of the answer or do they give a blanket response like "When they are not abusive anymore."

I would want to know what they felt were some of the underlying reasons a partner of the abuser normally allows the abuse to continue as long as it does. Do any of their answers strike some areas of truth within your own life?

Finally, I would ask what the number one attribute a couple needs to possess to successfully come out on the other side of abuse, while leaving the marriage intact. Their answer should give you a good indication whether they know what they are doing and whether they truly believe abuse is fixable and the marriage can flourish.

Do not be surprised if they ask you to come in for an initial consultation before answering any of these questions. That is okay. I would recommend pressing them on getting an answer to the couples counseling before agreeing to come in however.

I am strongly opposed to the notion that couples counseling can work, at least initially, when dealing with emotional abuse.

Chapter 21
Life Skills Program

It is good to be a part of life. Just as a sundial counts only the sunny hours, so does life know only that it is living. __H. G. Wells

Dr. Paul Hegstrom founded the Life Skills International program. Dr. Hegstrom was an emotional and physical abuser whom during an affair battered his girlfriend so severely that he was facing state attempted murder charges.

Instead of jail, he was given the opportunity to participate in a newly founded program for abusive men. After struggling initially, he went on to excel in the program and later took over the administration of it. Dr. Hegstrom remarried his first wife following a seven-year divorce and went on to study the science of the mind gaining his PhD.

Dr. Hegstrom and his wife Judy were also featured in a 1996 full-length movie for TV called "Unforgivable," which casts John Ritter as Dr. Hegstrom. It is quite a remarkable story and still amazes me how his battered wife could forgive and remarry him.

Just goes to show you - THERE IS HOPE!

You can find the movie on Amazon but it is cheaper to watch as an instant video. It is still not cheap but I believe it is a worthwhile investment. I was able to find the movie, broken into three parts, on YouTube, but have no idea whether the movie will still be available at the time you are reading this book.

You can search "Unforgivable (1966) John Ritter (1 of 3)" (quotes not needed) to find the first of the three parts.

At some point in time, Dr. Hegstrom started the Life Skills program, which features independent programs for both abusive people and those abused. A six-month program meets weekly. My class was three hours per week.

I was very blessed to be able to attend the Life Skills program in my own town. It helped me to understand the mysteries behind my abusive behavior and it helped me to understand that my abuse stemmed from wounding I suffered as a child.

I was able to unlock the mysteries of specifically how my abuse began. Having those mysteries revealed to me was the key to my getting healthy and my recovery. I took a second six-month class immediately following the first one for a total of one year of education in the psychology of abusive behavior.

I highly recommend the Life Skills program if it is offered near or close to your town, whether you are an abuser or being abused. You too will gain valuable education and practical tools to help you deal with your situation.

Please see the *Resources Section* for contact information.

I have listed the curriculum for the class below. As you can see, it is quite detailed and covers all aspects of the mind, human behavior, and how it all relates to family dynamics and abuse. You will also gain valuable insight on how to deal with other family members and how to effectively deal with conflict.

Curriculum

Dr. Hegstrom has kindly asked that the curriculum to his course be removed. Please contact his office for more information. You can visit the Life Skills International website at **http://www.lifeskillsintl.org/**. You may email them or call to find out if there is a Life Skills program in your area. Their email address is info@lifeskillsintl.org and their phone number is 303-340-0598.

Chapter 22
For the Abused

Every one of us, whatever our speculative opinions, knows better than he practices, and recognizes a better law than he obeys. __Foude

It is not your fault.

NOTHING you did, did not do, said, or did not say had any bearing on you being the victim of abuse. Take it from someone who spent 30-years trying to brainwash his wife into constantly second-guessing herself and wondering what she was doing wrong in the relationship to cause such problems in our marriage. There is *nothing* you did to cause your mates abusive trespasses into your mind, soul and psyche!

If you are in an abusive relationship, yet your mate doesn't feel they have a problem or they think the problem they have doesn't warrant seeing a counselor or enrolling in any other program, you still have a few options to consider.

You can research and find a counselor who has experience dealing with emotional abuse or you can attend a Life Skills program if one is offered in your area. They offer a six-month program for the abused as well as the abuser. See the *Resource Section* for contact information.

Regardless if you choose a classroom program or the services of a professional counselor, it is important that you acquire tools, knowledge, and methods to better understand and deal with your abusive situation. There may be issues from your childhood that need to be explored in order to discover how you fell into an abusive relationship.

Again, I am NOT saying it's your fault—it is not. But there may be underlying issues within you (codependency, unable to set boundaries, etc.) that caused you to stay in the relationship longer than you perhaps should have. Simply having a better understanding of exactly what is going on inside you will help.

Depending on the severity and length of time you have suffered with an abusive mate, you may want to consider removing yourself from the situation, especially if your mate is not claiming ownership of their abusive tendencies. What I am suggesting is removing yourself from the living situation you have with your abusive mate.

I realize this may not be easy, and the problem may be compounded if children are involved, but I believe staying under the same roof with someone who continues to abuse yet fails to accept any responsibility will not help the situation.

You, as the abused, must be willing to draw a hard line in the sand, to say "No more," and be willing to stick with your decision. It's very difficult, if not impossible, to do that while you're living under the same roof with your abusive mate. You must put separation and distance between you for the time being.

The underlying reason a person abuses is to control. Because, on the inside, an abuser is still a child, the 'outside' world to them is a scary place. They think they must control their surroundings in order to survive. Until you are willing to draw that hard line, they think they can still control you.

You must be willing to show you are done being controlled. This will hopefully serve as their wake-up call but that can only happen if you are willing to stand firm, separate yourself from them, and cut off *all* forms of communication – email, text, and phone calls, unless it involves your children, etc.

In my situation, it wasn't until Teri drew that line in the sand, and I knew she was serious, that I woke up and realized what I had to lose. In addition, that realization led to my discovery of the truth of who I was.

I'm not by any means suggesting that you file a formal separation and I'm certainly not suggesting that you seek a divorce. I'm suggesting that you merely remove yourself from the daily scourge of abuse and the constant pressure you feel by having to walk on eggshells around your mate. I am also suggesting you remove your children from that environment as well.

If you have the means and do move out for a period of time, be prepared for backlash from your mate. Again, their security depends on being able to control their surroundings and suddenly the person that means the most to them is attempting to remove themselves from their control. They are not going to be happy about that.

Just like a child, they will more than likely throw temper tantrums, threaten you, yell, scream, and generally come out fighting in an attempt to corral you back into their surroundings and control. I do not mean to minimize the impact of all the drama on you or your children, but the very fact they are showing that level of anger shows just how scared they are, and fear is a good motivator to change.

Once you make the decision to move out I encourage you not to move back in under *any* circumstance until you have had a period of time seeing evidence of *real change* in your mate. This certainly includes them accepting some form of responsibility and a willingness to seek outside counsel because they truly want to change. See the next chapter for specific information on *knowing* if your mate is truly changing.

They must be willing to do this even with you *not* moving back in; otherwise, it could simply be a ploy to get you back. As a test, find out how they react once they begin making changes in their life or make promises to you, only to find out that you are still not coming home, at least not yet.

Do they want to change because they realize they are broken or do they want to change simply to get you back?

I certainly do not know your situation, you, or your mate. I realize children can add another layer of complexity to the whole situation, especially if your mate is their father. So PLEASE don't take this as legal advice, but rather words of wisdom from someone who has been there, your mate needs a serious wake-up call.

Are you exposing yourself to any form of abuse from your mate in the process of him seeing his children? If so, I urge you to find some way for your children and their father to visit without you being in the middle. Perhaps a friend or family member would be willing to serve as an intermediary for a period.

Alternatively, perhaps that friend or family member would be willing to come over to where you live while your mate comes over to pick up the children. If possible, you could even send the children out to their father's car while you stay in the house.

The point is to make your mate realize their actions, and their actions alone have caused you to break off all contact with them — they must be willing to accept this fact. Acceptance means playing by your rules for a while; not that you are playing any kind of game with them, but they must come to the understanding that they no longer control you, the children, or their surroundings.

This will hopefully serve to put them in a very fearful place and they will come to the realization they must change in order to get back what they love the most, namely you.

Remember, your mate is probably an expert at the Jekyll-Hyde syndrome and can be quite charming when the need arises. That *charm* may even last for weeks at a time, but don't be fooled, especially if your mate has not taken any outside steps to get help. I can assure you they are unable to heal themselves, no matter how they appear.

I know all of this sounds easy for me to say on paper, but in all actuality is *very* difficult to do, even if there are no children involved. You must give the clear message that "enough is enough," and be willing to back that up with action that shows you are serious. Unfortunately in most cases, that's the only way your abusive mate will get the message.

It's a form of *tough love* I suppose and take it from me, until you draw that hard line in the sand, your mate has zero motivation to change and won't.

Do you continue in your relationship?

Only you can look inside your heart and determine if there is anything to hold on to. I realize it's a heart that has been laid out to your mate a thousand times only to be stomped on and shoved back in your chest, without the slightest bit of remorse or care.

No one but you can know the pain, the rejection, the unfulfilled hopes and dreams, and the number of times you've shown unconditional love only to be belittled, lied to, or rejected in return.

If I had the privilege of sitting at your kitchen table, sharing conversation and perhaps a cup of coffee or two, I would encourage you to take some time for yourself. Perhaps you are removed from your mate's oppressive environment, or maybe, after reading this book, you have more knowledge about abuse in general and your mate specifically.

Take some time to search your heart. I encourage you to try to shut off the noise in your head, be still, and listen. It will probably be a while before you hear anything, but in time, you will know what to do.

You have been part of an intimate, traumatic relationship for many, many years. I cannot imagine the number of wounds and scars that are hidden deep within your heart and soul. Because of it, I imagine you are not the same person you were before you entered this relationship. On the other hand, perhaps your previous relationship was not that much different from this one.

In any event, you need time to yourself in order to begin the healing process and to figure out what direction you would like to go.

As someone who was trapped for 30-years in the grip of abusive behavior, I can tell you with confidence that your mate is trapped in his or her own prison and they do not have a clue how they got there nor do they have a clue how to get out.

They were not born abusive and they did not wake up one day and say, "Gee, I think today I will be abusive." They do not realize the probable psychological trauma they suffered when they were a child that led to their abusive behavior.

I do not say this to condone or justify their behavior or actions for there is NO excuse for abuse!

However, there are underlying reasons they became abusive. In addition, once those reasons are understood and faced head-on, the control of abusive behavior can be neutralized and a healthy, loving behavior put in its place.

To this day, I thank my Lord that Teri had the courage to finally draw her own line in the sand. Her courage is what it took me to wake up. Her courage is what it took for me to get my life back after thirty-three years in a dark, dark abyss.

Though I wish she would have given it time, given *us* time (I know she'd LOVE the person I am today!), I understand and do not fault her for doing what she felt she had to do.

I would close out our conversation by giving you a hug and look into your eyes and say, "I am truly sorry for the pain you have endured over the past years. Your tender heart has been hardened, and no one knows but you and your Creator what you have had to endure.

I wish you well and the Lord's peace as you make decisions and face what I am sure will be a fearful future. You are a strong person to get this far, may your strength be renewed for what lies ahead."

I can assure you, it CAN and will get better. Good luck and may you find your way in the darkness. Remember, it is always the darkest, just before dawn!

Chapter 23
Is my Abusive Mate Changing?

When we are no longer able to change a situation - we are challenged to change ourselves. _Frankl

For the victim of emotional abuse, one of the hardest things to do, is to learn to trust again —especially their mate. The victims of abuse have had their entire soul and psyche messed with for so long, they begin to question their own sanity. Their self-confidence is shattered and many times, they don't know what to believe anymore.

Abusers are masters at deception. We can manipulate any conversation into so many twist, turns, branches, and dead ends, that it's hard for you to tell where the conversation started, where it currently rests, and even, what your last train of thought was.

We can make you think right is left, up is down, in is out, or *No* means *Maybe*... well, sometimes it does.

If your partner's eyes have been opened to their abusive ways, and they are committed to change, how do you know if the changes are real? How do you know they aren't yet another ploy or another deceptively charming mask, covering the same hideous beast of abusive behavior?

The short answer is, you don't—not initially at least. You have been lied to and had your hopes deflated more times than anyone will ever know, so its natural that confidence and trust in your mate will take time to be rebuilt. There are, however, some signs, or more accurately *behaviors,* that will signal real change is taking place.

The information presented below is gleaned from the pages of this book as well as a retrospective look at my own behavior the previous five years. I am confident what follows is not an exhaustive list; there may be other behaviors your mate exhibits that signal true change is occurring. However, I am equally confident that the behaviors listed below, are required if true and meaningful change is occurring.

It is important to realize your mate will have relapses from time-to-time during their journey to freedom from abuse. It will be difficult for you, during those relapses, to not panic and assume they are slipping back to who they were before. Be aware, your partner cannot possibly transition from being completely broken to healed in "one fell swoop," even if that's the desire of you both.

Evaluate the overall change you experience in your mate's behavior, attitude, and willingness to learn, rather than scoring on each of the listed categories. A recovering abuser may excel in one area yet lag in another for a period of time —months or years perhaps.

I encourage you to journal your daily experiences as you embark on this most challenging journey with your partner. Do not trust your memory, no matter how many times you tell yourself you will not forget. Record instances where your mate, in a given situation, might have acted one way in the past, yet now reacts in a different way —or at least tries to. It is easy to forget the small steps of recovery over time.

As the weeks melt into months and then years, you need reassurances that your mate's abusive behaviors are subsiding. This is the only way you can let your barriers down and begin to trust again.

Full Disclosure

Has your mate admitted their abusive behavior? Full disclosure of their behavior and a willingness to be transparent about their brokenness and remorse is where healing BEGINS.

No Excuses / Accept Responsibility

Your mate must quite making excuses for their behavior and begin to accept responsibility for their actions. Their arrested developed 'inner-child' will resist, it doesn't know how to accept responsibility. However, accepting responsibility and not making excuses is a sign your partner is emotionally maturing.

Blame

Blame goes hand-in-hand with excuses and not accepting responsibility. Your mate must stop blaming external circumstances or other people as a reason for their situation or behaviors.

Recompense

Are they making unselfish attempts to 'make amends' for their past behavior, without expecting a pay back? They should be willing to show how sorry they are, not just say it. Do they help out more around the house? Are they willing to 'take over' every once in a while so you can take a break?

Attitude

A change in attitude should be immediate and easy to detect. Are they able to openly talk and admit their past behaviors and/or admit and face the destructive attitudes they possessed during their years of abuse? Attitude will determine their ability to overcome obstacles along the road to recovery.

Realistic Viewpoint

Does you partner recognize and accept that their recovery will last for many years? Your partner must realize they are on a lifelong journey, rather than state they have reached their destination. Do they realistically look at the changes they have made are part of a "bigger picture" of recovery?

Conflict

Does your mate take appropriate action to de-escalate a heated discussion or argument? Do they call for a timeout, or respect your decision to call one? How does your mate respond to your anger or your criticisms of their behavior? During conflicts, do you notice that your mate's body language or facial expressions are different now as opposed to in the past? Do they continue to escalate their anger during the conflict, or do they at least make attempts to ratchet themselves down? An abuser, when attacked, will either attack back or withdrawal—do they exhibit the same type of "attack or withdrawal" they exhibited in the past, or are they attempting to break their old patterns? Does their language change for the worse? Do they bring up the past? Do they blame, make excuses, or refuse to accept responsibility?

Respect & Friendship

Is your mate showing a new level of respect to you? Are they more willing to listen to your side of the conversation without interrupting or interjecting his or her thoughts and beliefs? Do they respect your decisions, time, friends, or perhaps the way you choose to dress or style your hair? Just as one friend attempts to help out and edify another friend, your mate should want to help and edify you. Do they encourage you? Comfort you when you are struggling?

Equality of Power

Is there a more balanced level of power within the relationship? Is your input equal to their input? Decisions are made following valued input from both partners. Is there "give and take" in the relationship vs. all take as before?

Accepting Consequences

Does your mate realize he or she has no one else to blame for the situation they are in accept themselves? Do they feel sorry for *themselves* over what has happened, as in a "victim mentality" mindset? Do they show a willingness to move on, with a level of remorse in their heart?

Some of the areas mentioned above may place you in roles or situations that you are not comfortable with. You may not know how to deal with a balance of power or accept a new level of respect. The world you have been thrust into is just as foreign to you as the world your partner now finds themselves in. The difference is, you, more than likely, have zero trust and credibility built up in your partner's behavior.

Both of you must be willing to extend a lot of grace to each other during this transitional phase, as each of you learn to grow into your new skins, as it were. Trust is easily lost, yet difficult to regain. You have no reason or basis to trust your mate until he or she exhibits a prolonged and consistent attitude of change, and a willingness to accept responsibility for his or her past and present actions.

Perhaps your mate experienced a 'light bulb' moment similar to mine, and they have radically changed some of their behaviors almost overnight. Great! You, however, have not had such an experience, and therefore, can expect your changes and perceptions of your partner and your relationship to come at a much slower pace. That's okay. Give yourself the time you need.

You partner's acceptance of this fact, and a willingness to allow you to grow and change at your own pace and in your own way, is yet another sign of true and lasting change taking place.

Just as in the case of your partner, your recovery from abuse will take many years and you are under no obligation nor time frame to change, except as your heart allows.

Perhaps a good place to start with your recovery, is to learn to once again trust your instincts and intuition. If you have endured years of abuse, those instincts and intuitive thoughts have proven themselves false so many times, that you do not trust them anymore, or have learned to suppress them altogether.

I don't know your exact situation, but at some point, your intuition or instincts lead you to a realization that you were in an abusive relationship. They were correct in warning you of course, but you had a force – your mates abusive behavior – that overwhelmed and crushed those warning signals, or your ability to take action concerning them.

If you can find a way to once again trust those instincts and your intuition, ONLY as your mate proves his or her changes are real, than that may be a good place to start. Those instincts and intuition will serve you well as you move along *your* journey to recovery.

Chapter 24
The Best Helper I've Found

A man should never be ashamed to own he has been in the wrong, which is but saying, in other words, that he is wiser today than he was yesterday.
__Pope

I would not be doing my job if I did not mention my Lord and Savior, Jesus Christ, at this point in the book because frankly, I would not be where I am today without Him. Perhaps some of you reading this are feeling a pull in your heart to get to know Him too.

I spent two thirds of my life - thirty three years - stuck in an abusive cycle, one which I was being abused emotionally (totally unbeknownst to me) by my mother after my father died, and then as me being an abusive man, husband, and father to my family and others.

Thirty-three Years!

As I have stated in the book, my transition from being an abuser to being a *recovering* abuser happened within a matter of seconds. There is ZERO explanation for how that could happen without my Lord being involved in the process.

The road through recovery has been long, has been hard, and at times has been beset with setbacks. Yes, the old Austin has made an appearance from time to time.

If I had the opportunity to look you in the eyes I would say confidently that without Jesus, there is NO WAY I would have made it out of abuse successfully.

Maybe your mileage will vary, I don't know. I know of nine individuals who I have personally met and talked to that are also recovering abusers and every one of them is a Christian and following hard after Christ.

I am sure there are some non-Christians out there who have broken free as well but I am just saying that the ones I have *personally* talked to, all follow the Lord.

If you too are at a point where you *desperately* want to turn your life around and break free - TOTALLY FREE - of the prison of abuse BUT, just don't seem to be able to do it on your own, then I invite you to met the kindest, gentlest person I've ever had the privilege to meet; his name is Jesus Christ.

I'm not talking about a religion here. I'm not talking about 'church'. Some of the people who go there are a bunch of phonies and full of hypocrisy. I cannot stand those types of people!

No, I'm talking about a *relationship*. Just you and your Creator who very much wants to set you free from the lifestyle that you might have been locked into longer than I was locked into mine.

If you're desperate and simply don't know where to turn or have nowhere else to turn, I invite you to seek the Truth.

The Truth isn't some magic genie or fairy who's going to float down to your room and sprinkle fairy dust on you and POOF, you're all better. No, I am talking about someone who does not promise you it is going to be easy, He just promises He will be with you every step of the way.

He loves YOU with an unquenchable love! No matter what you have done or where you are at, right now, in your life!

If you would like to meet Jesus - and He is more than willing to meet you RIGHT where you are at - it is a simple process. No formal chant or even a specific prayer you have to say. You just have to talk from your heart, right now, right, where you are. And say something to the effect:

Tell Jesus you know you are a sinner, that you have not led a very good life up until this time.

Tell Jesus that you believe in your heart that He is the Son of God and that He came to earth to save people like you - sinners - by dying on a cross and conquering death when He rose from the dead.

You just have to ask Jesus to come into your heart to live, and to come into your heart and save you. To convert you from who you are to who He wants you to be. Tell him whatever else is on your heart that you need delivered from.

Whatever you feel, just say it, and allow Him to fill you with something you have never felt before —LIFE!

If you have said those words from a broken, repentant heart, I cannot promise that everything is going to be better over night—it probably will not, but you just might find yourself thinking or acting differently. You might find some of the things you really liked to do yesterday do not sound like much fun today; and those are all good things!

If you would send me an email - austin.f.james@gmail.com and tell me a little about your experience, I would sure appreciate it.

Welcome to the KINGDOM my friend!

Resources

Webliography

You can visit the life skills international website at *http://www.lifeskillsintl.org*. You may email them or call to find out if there is a Life Skills program your area. Their email address is info@lifeskillsintl.org and their phone number is 303-340-0598.

There is also a **Life Skills Youtube channel** (search "lifeskillsintl's channel" on Youtube) that might be worth watching. The videos on the channel are only samples of the videos for sale on the LSI website but they are still worth watching.

Bibliography

Breaking the Cycle of Abuse, Wiley; 1st Edition , December 2, 2005. How to Move beyond Your Past to Create an Abuse-Free Future, by Beverly Engel

The Emotionally Abusive Relationship: Wiley; 1st Edition, August 13, 2003. *How to Stop being Abused and How to Stop Abusing*, by Beverly Engel

The Jekyll and Hyde Syndrome: Wiley; 1st Edition, April 13, 2007. *What to Do If Someone in Your Life Has a Dual Personality - or If You Do*, by Beverly Engel

Note: I really like Beverly's writings. She has over 30-years experience working with clients who were emotionally, physically or sexually abused. She has experience! She was also abused in all three forms of abuse as a child, so she writes from a place of understanding.

Angry Men and the Women Who Love Them: Beacon Hill Press, 1st Edition, January 3, 2011.Breaking the Cycle of Physical and Emotional Abuse, by Paul Hegstrom

Broken Children, Grown-Up Pain (Revised): Beacon Hill Press, 2nd Edition, January 3, 2011. Understanding the Effects of Your Wounded Past, by Paul Hegstrom

Note: Dr. Hegstrom really gets into the psychology of our behaviors without getting to technical and over my head. Understanding the psychological reasons behind my behaviors allows me to internalize that I'm NOT defective in some way, as a person. That I can change once I reverse the patterns ingrained into my mind.

The Emotionally Destructive Relationship, House Publishers, August 15, 2007. Leslie Vernick

Why Does He Do That?: Berkley, September 2, 2003. Inside the Minds of Angry and Controlling Men, by Lundy Bancroft

Surrogate Husband Information

Since this form of abuse is very rare, here are some books you might want to check out pertaining to the subject. I have included a link to the Kindle version (if available) for each title.

Silently Seduced: *When Parents Make their Children Partners,* Understanding Covert Incest, by Kenneth M. Adams, Ph.D.

The Emotional Incest Syndrome: *What to do When a Parent's Love Rules Your Life*, by Dr. Patricia Love

When He's Married to Mom: *How to Help Mother-Enmeshed Men Open Their Hearts to True Love and Commitment*, Kenneth Adams and Alexander Morgan

Note: Notice there is not even any consistent terms within these three titles. It is very difficult to find information but perhaps "emotional incest" would be the best bet if you're trying to run a search on the Internet.

However, that form of abuse might lead quickly to the sexual aspect instead of the emotional

thank

you...

please

help

Thank you, please help...

I sincerely hope you have enjoyed this book and you were able to gather valuable insight into the mind of an emotional abuser as well as some practical knowledge that will help you.

I have a passion for stopping the destruction of emotional abuse BEFORE it has a chance to destroy yet another marriage and family, as well as the carnage it leaves in its path,

One way you can help me accomplish this, is to help me spread the word about emotional abuse and my experience with it. I believe as more former abusers are willing to come forward and admit our transgressions and discuss them, perhaps more people will become aware of this form of abuse and begin to seek help and healing for themselves.

As an independent (indie) author, I live and die by the reviews of my books. Not so much the rating of them - though higher ratings certainly help - but the quantity of them. Most people have an inherit reluctance to buy from an unknown author until they see what other people thought of the book.

To that end, would you assist me, and take a few moments to leave an honest review of what you read and perhaps how it impacted you —positive or negative?

I would sure appreciate it, and I thank you for your willingness to step forward in faith and purchase my book.

May God bless your journey and quite your soul.

Austin James

CPSIA information can be obtained at www.ICGtesting.com
Printed in the USA
LVOW13s2114270414

383445LV00029BA/708/P